CW00342807

First published 2011
by SelfMadeHero
A division of Metro Media Ltd
5 Upper Wimpole Street
London W1G 6BP
www.selfmadehero.com

Concept, Design and Copyright in the Work © SelfMadeHero, 2011
Recipe copyright © Josephine Bacon, 2011
The right of Josephine Bacon to be identified as the Author of this Work has been
asserted by her in accordance with the Copyright Designs and Patents Act 1988

Popeye and associated characters © 2011 King Features Syndicate, Inc.
™ Hearst Holdings, Inc.
™ King Features Syndicate, Inc.

Written by Josephine Bacon
Edited by Lorna Dunhill
Cover designed by Jeff Willis
Layout style by Andy Huckle
Editorial Assistant: Lizzie Kaye
Marketing Director: Doug Wallace
Publishing Director: Emma Hayley
With thanks to: Jane Laporte

All rights reserved. No portion of this book may be reproduced, stored in a retrieval
system, or transmitted in any form or by any means, mechanical, electronic,
photocopying, recording, or otherwise, without written permission from the publisher.

A CIP record for this book is available from the British Library

ISBN: 978-1-906838-37-9

10 9 8 7 6 5 4 3 2 1

Printed and bound in Slovenia

POPEYE cookbook

**RECIPES BY
JOSEPHINE BACON**

SELF MADE HERO

4

Popeye the Sailor man is an all-American hero, with a 36-ton capacity for his favourite muscle-building snack, spinach. **POPEYE'S SPINACH SPECIALS** (page 37) will ensure that you end up big and strong – just like Popeye!

Olive Oyl is Popeye's "sweetie patootie" with a talent for finding trouble. Luckily for Olive, Popeye is always ready with a can of spinach to rescue his damsel in distress! With her svelte figure, Olive Oyl is clearly a healthy eater, and **OLIVE OYL'S SALADS** from page 29 have lots of tasty recipes that she would love!

Swee'Pea is Popeye's ward and since being left in Popeye's protection (the very best there is!) Swee'Pea has learnt lots about fighting, but not so much about loving spinach. His favourite meals, all desserts, can be found in **SWEE'PEA'S SWEETS** from page 103.

Wimpy, or J. Wellington Wimpy to be precise, is a master con-artist and moocher, though certainly the most educated man of Popeye's acquaintance, with an IQ of 326. Despite 24 college degrees, Wimpy would rather just eat hamburgers than work. **WIMPY'S BBQ HAMBURGER** can be found on page 74.

Bluto is the constant thorn in Popeye's side – mostly as Olive Oyl is always having her head turned by this persistent brute! His tiny brain makes him no match for Popeye's spinach-boosted smarts, but his brawny body can withstand the knocks. For appetites like Bluto's, the **HEARTY MAINS** from page 45 are the order of the day.

HELLO!

My name is Josephine Bacon and, as you may be able to guess from my name, I am second cousin to Ham Gravy, who used to be Olive Oyl's boyfriend, but no hard feelings! We are all still good friends with Olive and with Popeye. Ham even contributed a recipe to this book – you can find it under **CITRUS-GLAZED HAM WITH BISCUITS AND RED-EYE GRAVY** (page 58).

The food in this book is the kind of food that Popeye likes – healthy, but not too healthy! That is to say, lots of healthy recipes along with a few that are just the kind of treat that people need now and again.

A question mark always hangs over "What is healthy?" of course. Take fats. Until a few years ago, butter was a total no-no and some cookery writers banned it from their vocabulary. Nutritionists have now decided that the real villains of the piece are "trans fats". Trans fats are fats that do not occur naturally and are usually solidified fats converted chemically from liquid fats such as oil. Everyone needs a certain amount of fat in their diet and, by making your own meals using the recipes in this book, you can control the amount of fats you eat as part of a balanced diet.

Apart from fried foods, especially those that are deep-fried, most people overindulge in fat in the form of mayonnaise or salad cream. This book includes a recipe for **YOGAISE** (page 140), made in the same way as mayonnaise, but replacing the oil with thick-set yogurt.

The healthiest foods contain large amounts of antioxidants. These are substances that destroy harmful substances in food and in your body. Powerful antioxidants include spinach and all red foods such as beetroot, red cabbage, raspberries – and, guess what? Dark chocolate! Yes, chocolate with a high percentage of cocoa solids is good for you!

One thing that all nutritionists agree on is that vegetables and fruits are the best part of the diet, which is why you are advised to eat at least five portions a day. If you find vegetables "boring", spice them up or include interesting additions, such as nuts or seeds. Raw vegetables are good for you, but sometimes cooking actually makes some of the nutrients available that cannot be absorbed when a vegetable is eaten raw. That is the case with tomatoes. Tomatoes contain an antioxidant called lycopene, more of which is absorbed from a cooked tomato than from a raw one, although raw tomatoes are higher in vitamin C.

Vitamin C is another essential in the diet. We are one of the few animals that does not make this vitamin ourselves but have to get it from an external source. Unfortunately, it is easily destroyed, not just by cooking but by long storage. That is why it is important to buy fresh fruits and vegetables and eat them as soon as possible after you get them home.

Naturally, since this is Popeye's book, it contains plenty of spinach recipes, for raw, cooked and tinned spinach. You may be surprised to learn that people in the Middle East and India, where spinach is a winter vegetable, eat much more spinach than we do. It is a favourite filling in all types of pastries.

I have tried to use simple recipes in this book but you will still need a few kitchen gadgets if they are to succeed. I have tried to use spoon measurements wherever possible as they are easier to measure than metric ones, but you will still need a kitchen scales for flour, for instance. You will also need a food processor, a blender, and several types of baking dishes and cake tins, round and square. When you are working with hot food or electrical kitchen equipment, it is always useful to have someone else present to help you.

Don't think you need to follow the recipes slavishly. First of all, you can always "cheat". For instance, if a recipe is given for the pastry for a pie, you can buy ready-made pastry dough at the supermarket. But try making pastry yourself when you are not too busy or pressured, just to see if you can do it. You will find that homemade tastes better in the end and you will know exactly what has gone into it.

It is entirely your choice how carefully you follow the recipe and if you think that, say, you would rather use hazelnuts than almonds or mango chutney instead of green chutney – go ahead! Your version may be tastier.

It is always best not to eat too much sugar and therefore where there is honey or sugar in a recipe feel free to use sugar substitutes, which can be bought in powdered or liquid form. You will need to follow the manufacturer's instructions for correct quantities.

I hope you like my choice of recipes – of course I consulted Popeye all the way, so they are his choice too.

Happy cooking and eating!

JOSEPHINE BACON

SOUPS & STARTERS

© King Features Syndicate, Inc., 1967. World rights reserved.

MELON MEDLEY

This looks best if the 2 types of melon are of different colours. Any leftover melon should be refrigerated immediately. A really ripe melon has a wonderful smell if you hold your nose close to it but unfortunately so many melons are refrigerated for long periods nowadays that by the time they get to the shops the scent has disappeared. This means it is hard to tell if a melon is ripe. If you have leftover watermelon, use balls of it too, but take out all the seeds first.

Serves 4
2 small charentais melons
1 small cantaloupe or ogen melon
8 tablespoons balsamic vinegar
4 sprigs fresh mint

Cut the small charentais melons in half crosswise. Scoop out and discard the seeds. Do the same with the cantaloupe or ogen melon. Use a melon baller to scoop out balls from the flesh of the cantaloupe or ogen melon. Pour the balsamic vinegar into a bowl and add the balls as you scoop them out. Then place 8 melon balls in each of the 4 charentais halves and pour over the balsamic vinegar, dividing it evenly between all 4 bowls. Add a sprig of mint to each melon "cup" to decorate.

CARROT CITRUS SALAD

This is a delicious starter, side-dish or salad. On a bed of lettuce with cottage cheese and crispbread it makes the perfect light lunch.

Serves 4
6 large carrots (about 750 g)
1 orange, juice squeezed
1 lemon, juice squeezed
2 teaspoons castor sugar (or to taste)
1 yellow grapefruit

Scrape the carrots thoroughly then grate them, using a coarse grater or coarse grating attachment on a food processor.

Squeeze the orange and lemon juice through a sieve (to remove the pips) into a bowl and mix it with the sugar. Taste for sweetness.

Peel the grapefruit, then remove the skin from the segments. Break the segments into pieces and discard any pips; add the grapefruit pieces to the grated carrots. Stir well to combine.

Cover the bowl with clingfilm and refrigerate for at least half an hour for the flavours to mingle.

MUSHROOM MARINADE

This recipe comes from Greece. Shop-bought mushrooms are perfectly safe to eat raw: they are grown in very sterile conditions.

Serves 6

750 g button mushrooms
2 beef tomatoes
2 tablespoons olive oil
1 bunch spring onions, trimmed, leaving 2.5 cm green parts
1 celery stick, diced
2 lemons, juice squeezed
1 orange, rind grated
2 sprigs thyme, 2 sprigs parsley and 1 bay leaf, tied together
2 large garlic cloves, chopped
1 tablespoon chopped fresh basil
1 tablespoon chopped fresh coriander
2 tablespoons coriander seeds
Salt and pepper
Fresh basil leaves

Bring 500 ml water to the boil and drop the tomatoes into it. Leave for 2 minutes then remove them with a slotted spoon and leave them to cool. When they are cool, skin them, cut in half and discard the pips then dice the flesh.

Wash the button mushrooms and slice any that are quite big. Sprinkle them with the juice of 1 lemon and reserve them in a bowl.

In a saucepan, heat the olive oil and add the onions, garlic, the bunch of herbs and the orange rind. When the oil bubbles continue cooking for around 3 minutes.

Add the tomatoes, the juice of the other lemon, the coriander seeds, salt and pepper. Cover and cook on low heat for 5 minutes.

Remove from the heat, add the sliced mushrooms, and leave to cool. Add the chopped basil and coriander. Stir well then transfer to a deep bowl and cover with clingfilm. Refrigerate until cold. Decorate with fresh basil leaves before serving.

Serve as a side-dish or a first course with warm crusty bread.

BABA GANOUSH

This recipe is sometimes called "poor man's caviar" – I have no idea why because it doesn't look or taste anything like fish roe! Aubergines grow well in the Mediterranean region. They are relatives of the tomato and the potato. When cutting away the stems, beware of the large prickles.

Serves 6
1.5 kg aubergines
1 tablespoon coarse salt
6 tablespoons extra-virgin olive oil
1 x 400 g tinned tomatoes
8 large black olives, stoned
1 tablespoon capers
1 teaspoon fresh basil, chopped
2 garlic cloves, finely chopped
1 teaspoon paprika, plus more for decoration
Parsley sprigs to decorate

Peel the aubergines and dice them into 2.5 cm cubes. Place them in a colander over a bowl and sprinkle them with the salt. Leave them for 1 hour for the liquid to drain out of them. Wipe the cubes dry with kitchen towels (and brush off any excess salt).

Heat the oil in a deep frying pan. Add the aubergine cubes and fry them, turning frequently, for 15 minutes. Slice the tomatoes and add them and their juice. Slice the olives and halve the capers and add them.

Reduce the heat and simmer for 10 minutes, or until the aubergine is soft and most of the liquid has evaporated. Add the basil and garlic and stir gently. Sprinkle with the paprika and cook for another 5 minutes.

Remove the mixture from the pan to a bowl to cool. When it is at room temperature, cover the bowl with clingfilm and refrigerate. Serve when cooled. If you can wait, it will taste even better the next day when the flavours have had a chance to mingle.

Serve in a salad bowl, decorated with parsley sprigs and a sprinkling of paprika. It is delicious with toasted pitta bread and raw dipping vegetables, such as carrots, cucumber, celery and peppers.

MUSHROOM PÂTÉ

The nice thing about this pâté is that it will taste different each time you make it, depending on the types of mushroom you use. If you pick mushrooms in the wild, wash them thoroughly and be sure you know what you are picking! Cultivated mushrooms need only be wiped with a damp cloth.

Makes 450 g
450 g cultivated flat mushrooms, porcini,
   oyster mushrooms or mixed wild mushrooms
225 g low-fat curd cheese
2 tablespoons thick-set yogurt
45 g unsalted butter
125 g chopped onion
1 teaspoon cracked black pepper
1 tablespoon freshly chopped parsley
1 tablespoon toasted pine nuts or toasted, blanched almonds

Clean the mushrooms and slice them, discarding the stalks. Melt the butter in a heavy-based pan and cook the onion until it is transparent. Add the mushrooms and cook for another 3 minutes or until they start to soften and give up their juice. Remove from heat and leave to cool for 10 minutes before adding the pepper.

Blend the curd cheese and yogurt in a blender. Add the mushroom mixture and parsley to the blender.

Blend on low speed to a smooth paste. Transfer to a small serving bowl, cover with clingfilm and refrigerate for at least 3 hours or overnight. Sprinkle with the nuts before serving.

The pâté will keep refrigerated for 5 days.

Serve with good crusty bread and salad leaves.

POPEYE'S SPINACH SPECIALS

SPINACH AND SCALLOP SALAD

This recipe is very simple and yet very delicious as an appetizer or side-dish. You could vary the shellfish by using cooked prawns, crabsticks, crayfish tails or fried cockles. You will need about 450 g for 4 servings.

Serves 4
1 tablespoon olive oil
8 scallops, white parts only, seasoned with salt and pepper
1 fennel bulb, chopped
600 g whole spinach leaves, trimmed and washed
1 lemon, rind grated, juice squeezed
2 tablespoons white wine vinegar
1 tablespoon walnut oil

Heat the oil in a frying pan and add the fennel and the scallops. Fry them for 1 ½ minutes on each side (overcooked scallops turn to rubber). Dry the spinach leaves on kitchen towels. Tear them into small pieces and place in a salad bowl. Add the cooked scallops and toss gently with the spinach. Sprinkle with the lemon juice, grated lemon rind, white wine vinegar and walnut oil.

SPINACH MUNKACZINA

This salad is Popeye's variation on the classic orange, onion and olive salad called Munkaczina (pronounced "Munkatchina") and it is vegetarian and easy-as-pie. It is particularly delicious if you use green olives stuffed with almonds or pimento. The perfect quick starter.

Serves 6
125 g black olives, stoned
125 g green olives, stoned
600 g baby spinach leaves, washed, trimmed and shredded
2 large red onions, sliced
2 navel or other seedless oranges, peeled and sliced
1 tablespoon extra-virgin olive oil

If the olives are large, you might want to cut them in half. Toss all the ingredients together in the order in which they are listed and put into a salad bowl. You could also add cubes of feta cheese. Serve as a starter with crusty bread.

SPINACH CHAAT WITH TAMARIND SAUCE

Chaat masala, sev, besan and chutneys can be found in any Indian grocery and in the ethnic foods shelves of good supermarkets.

Serves 8
8 potatoes, boiled
3 teaspoons ginger-and-green-chilli paste
3 teaspoons chaat masala
½ teaspoon sea salt
3 tablespoons besan (chickpea flour/gram flour)
16 whole spinach leaves, washed, stems trimmed
4 tablespoons peanut oil
100 g fresh coriander, chopped
250 ml plain thick-set yogurt
500 g gram flour noodles (known as *sev*)
8 tablespoons tamarind sauce

Mash the potatoes. Add the ginger-and-green-chilli paste, chaat masala, fresh coriander and salt.

Add a couple of tablespoons water to the besan (chickpea flour) to make a thick batter.

Spread a little potato mixture over 1 spinach leaf and cover with another spinach leaf. Press down tightly and fold into a tight, triangular package. Repeat with remaining leaves.

Dip the spinach leaf packages in the besan batter. Heat the oil in a large frying pan and fry the spinach packages (pakoras) until crisp. Drain them on kitchen paper.

Place a pakora on each plate. Add a mound of chopped coriander, some thick-set yogurt, some gram flour noodles and 1 tablespoon tamarind sauce and serve as a starter.

SPINACH WITH SUNFLOWER SEEDS

Any combination of nuts and seeds can be used. You could even try mixing the spinach with trail mix for a sweeter flavour.

Serves 6
900 g fresh spinach
½ teaspoon salt
½ teaspoon grated nutmeg
6 tablespoons shelled sunflower seeds
1 tablespoon grated coconut

Shake the spinach lightly after washing to ensure that most of the water remains on the leaves. Trim the stalks from the spinach and cut the bunches crossways and lengthways with a sharp knife.

Place the spinach in a saucepan and cover with a tight-fitting lid. Simmer for 5 minutes. Add the grated nutmeg and salt and cook for another 2 minutes. Transfer to a serving dish and sprinkle with the sunflower seeds and grated coconut.

SPINACH CHEESECAKE

This savoury cheesecake makes a delicious starter. It is quite rich so the portions are small. Serve it with a fresh tomato salsa (page 33) and a salad of sliced tomatoes, chopped onion and watercress.

Serves 8–10
175 g dry breadcrumbs
150 g ground almonds
200 g Cheddar or other hard cheese, finely grated
75 g butter, softened
100 g fresh spinach, coarsely chopped
3 garlic cloves, peeled and cut in half
½ teaspoon sea salt
½ teaspoon freshly ground black pepper
75 ml thick-set yogurt
900 g cream cheese, softened
3 eggs
50 ml milk
Garnish with walnut halves and sprigs of watercress

Combine the breadcrumbs, ground almonds, cheese and butter. Use the mixture to line the bottom of a 20 cm springform tin to a depth of 2.5 cm.

Place the spinach in a food processor and add the garlic, salt and pepper. Process until smooth then, with the processor running, pour the yogurt through the hole in the top in a steady stream until mixture is blended.

Put the cream cheese in another bowl. Use the food processor or a stick blender to blend the cream cheese until light and fluffy. Add the eggs, one at a time, beating well after each addition. Add the milk, then blend in the spinach mixture, mixing well.

Preheat the oven to 160°C/Gas Mark 3.

Pour the mixture into the prepared tin. Bake for 1 hour then turn off the oven and wedge open the door with a wooden spoon. Leave the cheesecake in the oven for 1 hour to set.

Remove the cheesecake and let it cool to room temperature before unmoulding it. Cover it and chill until required. Garnish just before serving with walnuts halves and sprigs of watercress.

POPEYE'S ITALIAN-STYLE SPINACH

Serves 6
900 g fresh spinach
½ lemon, juice squeezed
4 garlic cloves, chopped
6 tablespoons pine nuts
½ teaspoon grated nutmeg

Shake the spinach lightly after washing to ensure that most of the water remains on the leaves. Trim the stalks from the spinach and cut the bunches crossways and lengthways with a sharp knife.

Put the garlic cloves in a saucepan and add the spinach. Cover with a lid and simmer for 5 minutes.

Place the pine nuts in a dry non-stick frying pan and toast, stirring and watching carefully to ensure they brown evenly and are not allowed to blacken. Remove them from the heat.

Stir the pine nuts into the spinach, add the lemon juice and the grated nutmeg and stir well. Serve immediately.

SPINACH À LA MODE

This is the perfect recipe for a boiling hot summer day – Parmesan ice cream with cold spinach!

Serves 4
250 g Parmesan cheese, finely grated
400 ml thick-set, low-fat plain yogurt
2 egg whites
600 g fresh spinach, trimmed and well washed
½ lemon, juice squeezed
2 teaspoons castor sugar (or to taste)
2 nashi pears (we call these Asian pears)

Combine 150 g of the Parmesan and 200 ml of the yogurt and set aside in a warm place for 30 minutes or until the Parmesan has come to room temperature.

Whisk the egg whites into soft peaks, add the rest of the yogurt and whisk until firm. Stir the rest of the Parmesan into the softened mixture and fold the stiffly whipped mixture into it.

Pour the mixture into a plastic container with a lid and freeze for at least 2 hours or until required.

Meanwhile cook the spinach in its own rinsing water with the lemon juice and remove from the heat. Chop finely and add the sugar. Cool, then chill it.

To serve, cut the nashi pears into halves, core them and fill the scooped out centres with the spinach. Serve with 2 scoops of Parmesan ice cream as an unusual main course.

HEARTY
MAINS

LEMON AND OLIVE CHICKEN

This is a favourite Moroccan dish. Serve it with couscous or rice and a watercress salad.

Serves 6
1 roasting chicken (about 1.6 kg), cut into serving pieces
3 saffron strands
4 tablespoons olive oil
175 g green olives, stoned
2 lemons
4 garlic cloves, peeled and chopped
2 bay leaves
4 tablespoons chopped flat-leaved parsley

Dilute the saffron in 1 tablespoon warm water and brush it over the chicken. Brush the pieces of chicken with the olive oil. Place the chicken pieces in a large heavy saucepan with a tight-fitting lid.

Slice the lemons and arrange them over the chicken pieces then sprinkle with the olives, garlic, bay leaves and parsley. Add water to cover (about 1 litre) and simmer for 1 hour. Serve immediately.

LIME AND MANGO CHICKEN

Chicken with a touch of the Orient found by Popeye in the Islands. This exotic recipe is simplicity itself. You can also fry or grill the marinaded chicken pieces, reserving the marinade, heating it and serving it as a sauce. The chicken will also barbecue nicely.

Serves 6
1 medium chicken, cut into serving pieces
1 mango
2 limes, rind grated, juice squeezed
2 tablespoons soy sauce
1 tablespoon extra-virgin olive oil
1 teaspoon freshly ground black pepper
1 teaspoon sweet paprika
1 teaspoon ground allspice
4 tablespoons runny honey
1 bay leaf
1 onion stuck with 2 whole cloves

Arrange the pieces of chicken in a shallow bowl. Peel the mango, cut into slices and discard the seed. Place the slices of mango over the chicken. Mix all the other ingredients together, except the bay leaf and onion, in the order of listing. Pour the liquid over the chicken and leave overnight to marinate.

The next day, transfer the chicken and marinade to a casserole dish. Add the bay leaf and onion stuck with cloves, then add water to cover. Cover the casserole with a lid. Heat the oven to 180°C/Gas Mark 4 and put the chicken in to bake. Bake for 1–1 ½ hours. Serve with plain boiled rice and boiled leeks. If you barbecue the chicken, serve with one of Olive Oyl's salads.

SESAME CHICKEN LEGS

Serve with a green vegetable such as spinach or with jacket potatoes or baked sweet potatoes. Garnish with a green salad or with watercress.

Serves 6
12 chicken legs
2 eggs, beaten
2 tablespoons soy sauce
125 g wholewheat flour
175 g sesame seeds
2 teaspoons paprika
1 teaspoon sea salt
4 tablespoons sunflower or rapeseed oil

Combine the beaten egg with the soy sauce and pour into a shallow bowl. In another shallow bowl, combine the wholewheat flour, sesame seeds, paprika and salt. Dip each leg thoroughly in the beaten egg mixture then roll it in the flour and sesame seeds mixture.

Put the oil in a frying pan. Heat the oil until a little of the flour mixture dropped into the pan bubbles instantly. Fry the chicken legs in 2 batches, turning until evenly browned. Drain on kitchen towels.

Preheat the oven to 180°C/Gas Mark 4. Transfer the chicken legs to a baking dish and bake, uncovered, for 30 minutes. Serve immediately.

CHICKEN CACCIATORE

The translation of the name of this Italian recipe is "hunter's chicken" because the hunter brought the chicken with him and then found hedgerow herbs and fungi with which to cook it. It was a quick and easy meal prepared over a camp fire or on board ship. The essential ingredients are tomatoes and mushrooms (cultivated or wild) but you can add any herbs you like. Like so many stews, this dish is best prepared the previous day and reheated when required.

Serves 6
1 large chicken, about 1.5–2 kg, jointed
4 tablespoons olive oil
2 garlic cloves, chopped
4 large flat mushrooms, sliced
425 ml passata
2 x 400 g tinned tomatoes, tomatoes sliced, juice reserved
1 teaspoon dried basil
1 teaspoon dried oregano
2 teaspoons dried or fresh chopped parsley
½ teaspoon sea salt
¼ teaspoon cayenne pepper
2 tablespoons potato flour
4 tablespoons chicken stock

Heat the oil in a deep pot or casserole. Add the chicken pieces and brown them all over, removing them to kitchen towels to drain. Replace them with the garlic and mushrooms and cook, stirring, until they start to give up their juice, about 5 minutes. Return the chicken to the pot and cover it with the passata, tinned tomatoes with their juice, basil, oregano, parsley, sea salt and cayenne pepper.

Cover the pot, reduce the heat and simmer for 45 minutes or until chicken is tender. Mix the potato flour with the chicken stock; stir until smooth, then stir this into the sauce. Continue cooking for 10 minutes or until the sauce is thick and bubbly. Remove from the heat and serve or leave to cool, then refrigerate overnight.

Serve Chicken Cacciatore with shell pasta (conchiglie) or rigatoni to soak up the sauce.

NASI GORENG
POPEYE'S FAVOURITE DISH FROM THE ORIENT

This is one of Popeye's favourites from his trips to Indonesia. Nasi Goreng just means "fried rice" in the local language, Bahasa Indonesia, but it has all kinds of delicious accompaniments and dipping sauces. Nowadays, *kecap manis* and *sambal oelek* are easy to source at big supermarkets or oriental grocers. Like so many dishes from this part of South-East Asia, the food is served lukewarm, never piping hot. You can use leftover rice or rice cooked the night before. It is the custom in Indonesia to serve the rice dish with sambals, little bowls or dishes of dipping sauces.

Serves 6

350 g long-grain or jasmine rice
4 tablespoons rapeseed oil
3 eggs, beaten
2 small green chilli peppers, seeded and chopped
1 leek, trimmed and chopped
1 garlic clove, finely chopped
2 onions, 1 finely chopped, 1 sliced into thin rings
2 tablespoons blanched, slivered almonds
1 teaspoon ground coriander
1 teaspoon ground cumin
250 g chicken breast
250 g cooked, peeled prawns
3 tablespoons kecap manis
2 tablespoons sambal oelek
More kecap manis for dipping
More sambal oelek for dipping
1 lime, juice squeezed, rind grated

Cook the rice in 3 times its volume of water, until tender (about 20 minutes). Leave it to cool until cold.

Beat the eggs. Heat 1 tablespoon of the oil in a frying pan and make an omelette. When cooked, cut the omelette into narrow strips and reserve them.

Heat 1 tablespoon of oil in the pan in which the omelette was cooked and cook the onion rings until they are nicely browned. Take them from the pan and reserve. Replace them with the almonds and toast the almonds until lightly browned. Remove them from the pan and reserve them on kitchen towels.

Heat 2 tablespoons of the oil in a wok or large frying pan. Add the chopped onion, leek, garlic and chilli peppers, fry until soft, then add the coriander and cumin. Slice the chicken breast into strips and add it with the prawns to the onion mixture and cook, stirring occasionally, for 5 minutes. Add the rice, kecap manis, sambal oelek and omelette strips and cook for a further 5 minutes.

Mound the mixture on a large serving dish. Sprinkle with the onion rings, almonds and grated lime rind.

Pour the additional kecap manis into a small bowl for serving separately and do the same with the lime juice and the extra sambal oelek. These are the sambals.

CHICKEN BREASTS IN APRICOT MARINADE

Apricots have a very short season, just late May to early July, and this is a perfect way to take advantage of them, especially as they are not always particularly ripe or sweet when they reach the shops. At other times of year, use dried apricots: you will only need half the amount, i.e. 450 g.

Serves 8
8 chicken breasts, skinned

For the apricot marinade:
4 oranges, juice squeezed
1 teaspoon garlic salt
2 garlic cloves, peeled and chopped
½ teaspoon freshly ground black pepper
1 tablespoon demerara sugar
3 tablespoons cider vinegar
5 cm root ginger, peeled and cut into matchstick strips
900 g fresh apricots, stoned and halved
1 tablespoon extra-virgin olive oil

In a large saucepan, cook the orange juice with the garlic salt, garlic cloves, pepper, sugar, cider vinegar, root ginger and apricots. Bring to the boil and cook for 5 minutes. Remove from the heat and leave to cool. When cool, place the ingredients with the olive oil in a blender and blend until smooth.

Pour this marinade into a shallow bowl. Cut the chicken breasts in half and place them in the marinade. Marinate for at least 2 hours or overnight in the refrigerator.

Heat the oven to 190°C/Gas Mark 5. Arrange the chicken pieces in a roasting tin and pour the marinade over them. Bake for 30 minutes. Serve with plain boiled rice and a green vegetable.

POPEYE'S FAVOURITE POACHED CHICKEN WITH EGG-AND-LEMON SAUCE

Although poached chicken does not look as attractive as roast chicken, it is juicy and delicious, and has a lower fat content as it can be cooked without the skin. For boiled chicken you need an older bird since it has more flavour. The best boiling fowl are to be found at halal butchers. Serve with boiled rice and a green vegetable.

Serves 6
1 x 2.5 kg boiling fowl, cut into 6 pieces
6 flat-leaved parsley sprigs
½ lemon, skin thoroughly scrubbed
1 small turnip, halved
½ teaspoon salt
2 garlic cloves, peeled
2 celery sticks

For the egg and lemon sauce:
2 lemons, thoroughly scrubbed
1 tablespoon potato flour or cornflour
2 egg yolks, beaten
½ teaspoon salt

Remove as much fat as possible from the chicken (most of it is at the rear end) and as much skin as possible. Discard the skin. Put the chicken in a large casserole dish or deep pot with a lid. Add water to just cover the chicken and add the parsley sprigs, ½ lemon and turnip. Bring the water to the boil over medium-high heat and add the salt, garlic and celery. Cook, skimming off any scum that rises to the surface, for 10 minutes.

Reduce the heat to low, cover the pot, and simmer the chicken for 1 ½ hours or until tender. Remove the chicken from the pot and arrange on a serving platter. Reserve in a warm place while you make the sauce.

Strain the cooking liquid and allow to cool to room temperature. Skim the fat that rises to the surface with kitchen towels. Reheat the cooking liquid and boil, uncovered, for 15 minutes to reduce it.

Meanwhile, grate 1 lemon and add the rind to the cooking liquid. Squeeze the juice from both lemons, using a lemon squeezer, and mix it with the potato flour or cornflour and the salt. Stir until smooth. Remove the cooking liquid from the heat and stir the thickened lemon juice into it. Allow to cool slightly.

Pour the liquid into a heatproof bowl, such as a pudding basin, or the top part of a double boiler. Beat the yolks into the liquid until smooth. Add the salt. Pour boiling water into a pan or the lower part of a double boiler and place on low heat. Place the pudding basin or top part of the boiler and cook over the water, stirring constantly, until the liquid coats the back of a spoon.

Pour the sauce over the chicken and serve immediately.

SHIPMATES' ORANGE CHICKEN

When you cook with the rind of an orange or lemon it should preferable be untreated, i.e. not sprayed with chemicals or waxed. Whether it is untreated or not, it must be washed thoroughly before use.

Serves 6
1 chicken (about 2.5 kg)
1 whole untreated sweet or blood orange
1 teaspoon ground cloves
4 tablespoons orange juice
2 large onions

Wash the chicken thoroughly. Pour boiling water through the cavity and place the whole orange in the cavity. Cut one of the onions into quarters.

Preheat the oven to 190°C/Gas Mark 5.

Place the chicken and onion quarters in a roasting pan, preferably on a trivet so the bottom does not touch the liquid. Mix the ground cloves with the orange juice and pour the mixture over the chicken. Then grate the other onion and pour the grated onion and juice over the chicken.

Roast the chicken for half an hour then reduce the oven temperature to 180°C/Gas Mark 4 and roast for another hour. Baste the chicken with the juices every 15 minutes.

When serving, cut the orange inside the chicken into as many serving pieces as there are diners and serve it on the side.

Serve with rice and spinach.

CHICKEN POT PIE

Although this pie looks like a lot of work, all the preparation can be performed in advance. The dough can be made the night before and refrigerated until required (see page 141 on how to make a savoury pastry). The chicken breasts can be cooked the night before or you could even cook all the filling the night before. This makes a delicious Sunday lunch, served with steamed carrots and spinach with pine nuts (page 43) or sunflower seeds (page 41).

Serves 6
For the filling:
6 chicken breasts, bone-in, skin-on
4 medium carrots
salt
freshly ground black pepper
1 litre chicken stock
25 g unsalted butter
2 small onions, chopped
2 leeks, trimmed and sliced into 2 ½ cm slices
120 g plain flour
4 tablespoons low-fat crème fraîche
300 g frozen peas
250 g pearl onions, fresh and peeled or frozen
4 tablespoons chopped parsley

For the dough:
375 g plain flour
½ teaspoon salt
1 teaspoon baking powder
125 g suet or lard
120 g cold unsalted butter, diced
About 200 ml iced water
1 egg beaten with 1 tablespoon water

Preheat the oven to 180°C/Gas Mark 4.

To make the filling, place the chicken breasts on a baking sheet and season with salt and pepper. Bake them for 35 minutes. While the chicken is baking, bring a saucepan of water to the boil and add the carrots. Parboil them for 10 minutes, then drain them and leave them to cool. Remove the chicken from the oven and leave to cool. Then remove the meat from the bone and cut into large dice. Dice the carrots. Reserve the chicken and carrots.

In a flameproof casserole dish, melt the butter and fry the onions and leeks over medium-low heat for 10 to 15 minutes, until translucent. Add the flour and cook over low heat, stirring constantly, for 5 minutes, while you heat the chicken stock. Pour the hot, but not boiling, stock into the onion mixture and cook, stirring until the liquid thickens. Stir in the crème fraîche, diced chicken, diced carrots, peas, pearl onions and parsley. Mix well.

Make the dough using the ingredients listed here, and the method on page 141. On a floured board knead the dough briefly and roll it out. Wrap it in clingfilm and refrigerate for at least 1 hour. Preheat the oven to 200°C/Gas Mark 6.

Divide the filling equally among 6 ovenproof bowls. Divide the dough into 6 pieces and roll each piece into a 20 cm circle. Brush the rim of each bowl with the egg-and-water mixture, then cover each bowl with a round of dough. Trim the round of dough to 1 cm wider than the rim of the bowl. Press the dough firmly over the rim of each bowl, and brush it all over with the egg wash. Make a slit in the centre of each dough circle. Place the bowls on a baking sheet and bake for 1 hour, or until the pastry is golden brown. Serve immediately.

PERSIAN POMEGRANATE CHICKEN

Pomegranates are all the rage for their healthiness at the moment. This Persian recipe can be used for cooking any kind of poultry or game instead of the chicken breasts. Ideally, it is made with pomegranate molasses which can be found in Persian food shops. If you are lucky enough to find it, use it instead of the black treacle.

Serves 4
200 g walnut halves
2 tablespoons honey
250 ml pomegranate juice, freshly squeezed if possible, seeds strained out
1 tablespoon black treacle
2 tablespoons olive oil
1 onion, finely chopped
½ teaspoon freshly ground black pepper
½ teaspoon ground turmeric or saffron threads
4 large chicken breasts, skinned, boned and sliced
1 tablespoon potato flour
2 limes, juice squeezed
½ teaspoon coarse salt
1 ½ teaspoons ground cardamom

Toast the walnuts in a dry frying pan until they begin to give off an aroma. Remove from the pan and chop them (if using a food processor, be careful not to chop them too finely until they melt into a butter). Combine them with half the honey and return to them to the pan. Cook, stirring constantly, for 2 minutes, then set aside.

Pour the pomegranate juice into a saucepan and bring it to the boil. Reduce the heat and cook uncovered until it has reduced by half. Stir in the treacle and cook for 2 minutes. Remove from the heat and set aside.

In a large, deep frying pan, heat half the oil and add the onion, black pepper and turmeric or saffron. Cook the onion until it is nicely browned, about 7 minutes.

Preheat the oven to 175°C/Gas Mark 4. Oil a casserole dish and place the chicken breast slices in it. Sprinkle the chicken breasts with the reduced pomegranate liquid then sprinkle with the potato flour, lime juice, chopped walnuts and coarse salt. Cover with the onion mixture. Cover the casserole with a lid and bake for 45 minutes. Then add the ground cardamom and cook for a further 10 minutes.

Serve with Persian Spinach Rice (page 100).

CHICKEN SUPREME

The cut of chicken known as "suprême" in French is the breast and the first segment of the wing. Supreme sauce, however, is a white sauce flavoured with bacon. You can use supremes or simply breast of chicken for this recipe.

Serves 6
3 rashers back bacon, rinds removed
2 tablespoons olive oil
2 onions, sliced
4 garlic cloves, chopped
6 supremes or breasts of chicken, skinned and boned, cut into slices
2 tablespoons chopped parsley
125 ml chicken stock
400 ml low-fat cream
Salt and freshly ground black pepper

Heat a deep non-stick pan or wok with a lid and add the bacon. Cook until the bacon fat melts and the bacon is crispy. Remove it from the pan and drain it on kitchen towels. If there is not enough bacon fat add 1 tablespoon oil. Add the onion and garlic and fry until the onion is soft and transparent.

Add the rest of the oil to the pan, heat it and add the chicken slices. Cook them through, shaking and stirring the pan occasionally, until they are lightly browned all over, about 10 minutes. Return the onion and garlic to the pan with the chopped parsley and cook for 2 minutes. Add the chicken stock and cream and stir until the chicken breasts are coated, and the liquid is hot – but do not let it boil. Add salt and pepper to taste.

Serve on a bed of white rice or inside a Spinach and Rice Ring (page 99).

ORANGE-GLAZED PORK CHOPS
WITH ORANGE DIPPING SAUCE

Serve these pork chops with plain boiled rice. A mixture of wild rice and long-grain will make it a special meal. Cooked spinach is a great accompaniment.

Serves 4
4 pork chops, fat trimmed about 2 cm thick
1 tablespoon olive oil
½ teaspoon salt
½ teaspoon freshly ground black pepper
2 oranges, freshly squeezed, 1 rind finely grated
2 tablespoons muscovado sugar
2 tablespoons orange marmalade
1 tablespoon balsamic vinegar
Pinch of cinnamon
1 tablespoon soy sauce

In a large heavy-based frying pan with a lid heat the olive oil. Brown the pork chops on both sides in hot oil, about 5 minutes on each side. When cooked, season pork chops with salt and pepper and place them on kitchen towel to drain. Drain excess fat from the frying pan.

In a bowl, combine half the orange juice, grated rind, muscovado sugar, marmalade, balsamic vinegar and pinch of cinnamon. Return the chops to the pan and pour the orange mixture over them. Cover the pan and simmer for 45 minutes, turning once to ensure both sides are glazed.

Meanwhile add the soy sauce to the reserved orange juice and pour it into a small bowl.

When the chops are cooked, serve them and hand the dipping sauce round with them.

CITRUS-GLAZED HAM
WITH BISCUITS AND RED-EYE GRAVY

This is a typical recipe from the American Deep South. The "biscuits" are not biscuits at all but a sort of scone, for which the recipe is on page 59. Bake the biscuits in the same oven as the ham so they are ready together.

It is often important to soak a ham in water overnight in the fridge to remove the salty brine. Check with your butcher or on the label.

Serves 10–12
Citrus-glazed Ham:
1 small whole bone-in raw ham (about 3 kg)
10 whole cloves
3 ruby grapefruit

Red-eye Gravy:
1 tablespoon arrowroot
125 ml water
250 ml cider vinegar
125 ml runny honey
250 ml strong coffee
1½ tablespoons muscovado sugar
½ teaspoon freshly ground black pepper
¼ teaspoon hot pepper sauce

To serve: American biscuits

Preheat the oven to 180°C/Gas Mark 4.

Place the ham in a deep roasting tin, fat side upwards and bake it for 90 minutes. Remove it from the oven and increase the oven temperature to 190°C/Gas Mark 5. Carefully skin the ham, discard the skin and, with a sharp knife, score the fat into diamonds. Place a clove in the centre of 10 of the diamonds.

Squeeze the juice from 2 of the grapefruit and combine it with the cider vinegar and honey. Pour the liquid over the ham and return the ham to the oven. Bake for 40 minutes, basting every 10 minutes with the cooking liquid.

While the ham is cooking, peel the third grapefruit and remove as much of the pith and connective tissue as possible. Remove the skin between the segments.

Remove the ham from the oven and transfer it to a serving dish. Place the roasting tin on the stove and use the liquid to make the Red-eye gravy. Combine the arrowroot and water. Add the coffee, sugar, pepper and hot sauce to the pan and stir well to dislodge any bits that may have stuck to the bottom until the liquid thickens. Add the dissolved arrowroot and stir until thickened and boiling. Arrange the segments of the third grapefruit around the ham. Pour half the liquid over the ham and serve the rest separately.

Serve with the biscuits and a vegetable, such as spinach.

AMERICAN BEATEN BISCUITS

I like to use goat's milk yogurt as a substitute for the buttermilk, to make these scones. You may find the flavour of this yogurt too "goaty". If you don't like goat's milk, try and make your own buttermilk (page 14).

Makes 8 biscuits (double the quantities for serving with the recipe opposite)
250 g plain flour
¼ teaspoon salt
½ teaspoon baking powder
1 tablespoon sugar
50 g lard, chilled and cut into small pieces
75 ml plain yogurt or buttermilk (recipe page 14)

Sift flour, salt, baking powder and sugar together. Use a food processor to cut the lard into the flour until it resembles breadcrumbs. Beat the dough as you slowly add the yogurt. Mix well until the dough coheres into a ball, adding a tablespoon or two of water if needed.

Knead the dough for 3 minutes then wrap it in plastic and refrigerate for 1 hour. Roll out the dough into a rectangle, beating it with a rolling pin. Fold half the dough over the other half, then beat it again. Repeat this process until the dough turns white and blisters form on the surface. It should take about 15 minutes. Get someone to help you if you feel tired (children love doing this).

Preheat the oven to 230°C/Gas Mark 8. Line 2 baking sheets with non-stick baking paper.

Roll out the dough to about 5 mm thick and use a fluted biscuit cutter to cut it into 5 cm rounds. Prick the top of each biscuit a few times with the tines of a fork. Place on the lined baking sheets. Bake the biscuits for 15 minutes, or until pale golden. Serve hot.

TURKEY MOLÉ

The turkey is a native American bird and it is eaten every day of the year in the USA. It is particularly associated not with Christmas as in Europe, but with Thanksgiving, the secular holiday that is celebrated in the United States on the 4th Thursday in November. It is to honour the native peoples who greeted the newcomers when they reached Plymouth Rock in Massachusetts. It was first celebrated in 1621. The traditional meal consists of a mixture of local foods and those the settlers brought with them, and turkey is usually the main course. Unsweetened chocolate can be found in Caribbean grocers or use plain chocolate containing as little sugar as possible. This typically Mexican turkey dish is believed to have been invented by Mexican nuns.

Serves 8–10
1 turkey (about 4.5 kg), cut into pieces, with giblets
2 onions, peeled and halved
2 carrots, scraped and split
3 celery sticks
½ teaspoon sea salt
2 bay leaves
10 black peppercorns
5 allspice berries

Molé Sauce:
6 tablespoons Mexican chilli powder
6 tablespoons toasted sesame seeds
2 tablespoons blanched almonds, split
50 g corn tortilla chips, broken into pieces
125 g raisins
2 garlic cloves, peeled and chopped
½ teaspoon aniseed
1 teaspoon ground cinnamon
½ teaspoon ground cloves
½ teaspoon ground coriander
3 very ripe tomatoes, skinned and chopped

3 shallots, finely chopped
45 g unsweetened chocolate, grated
2 tablespoons olive oil
2 tablespoons chopped parsley
Extra sesame seeds for sprinkling

In a large flameproof casserole, combine the turkey pieces and giblets with the onions, carrots and celery sticks. Add enough water to cover by 5 cm and bring to the boil, skimming off any scum that rises to the surface. When boiling, add the salt, bay leaves, peppercorns and allspice and reduce the heat. Cover and simmer for 45 minutes.

Remove the turkey pieces from the pot, reserving the liquid, and place them on a chopping board. Separate the meat neatly from the bones and return the bones to the pot. Put the meat to one side.

WELSH LAMB WITH POTATOES AND PEAS

Breast of lamb is a cheap cut but very fatty. Make sure you roast it in a pan on a trivet so that it does not sit in its own fat.

Serves 6–8
1 breast of lamb (about 1.8 kg)
1 tablespoon chopped rosemary
4 rosemary sprigs
8 mint sprigs
½ teaspoon salt
½ teaspoon freshly ground black pepper
12 new potatoes
450 g frozen peas
Salt and pepper

Remove the lamb from the refrigerator, cover it with a cloth and leave until it is at room temperature. Preheat the oven to 200°C/ Gas Mark 6.

Sprinkle the lamb with the chopped rosemary, salt and pepper. Place it on a trivet in a roasting pan and add 250 ml cold water to the pan. Add the rosemary sprigs and 4 of the mint sprigs to the water. Roast the lamb for 30 minutes, then remove the pan from the oven. Add the new potatoes around the lamb, add another 125 ml water if the liquid has dried up and return the meat and potatoes to the oven.

Roast for another 30–45 minutes. Meanwhile, heat 250 ml water in a saucepan with the remaining mint sprigs. Add the peas and bring to the boil. Boil for 2 minutes. Serve the lamb on a roasting dish with the potatoes and peas mixed together in a vegetable dish. Discard the mint and season the meat with salt and pepper before serving.

BLUTO'S BAKED LAMB SHANKS
WITH BALSAMIC VINEGAR

Lamb shanks require slow cooking, preferably with parboiling, tightly wrapped in cloth to boil away the excess fat. You can also leave out this stage and cook the meat until done then leave it to cool and refrigerate overnight. Skim off the fat, reheat and serve the next day.

Serves 2

2 lamb shanks, about 900 g
2 tablespoons olive oil
½ teaspoon salt
½ teaspoon freshly ground black pepper
3 rosemary sprigs
4 celery sticks, roughly chopped
2 onions, 1 chopped, 1 quartered
2 tablespoons tomato purée
250 ml balsamic vinegar
750 ml beef stock
2 tablespoons freshly chopped parsley
2 garlic cloves, crushed

Wrap the lamb shanks tightly in muslin (cheesecloth) and place in boiling water. Bring to the boil and simmer for 30 minutes. Remove from the pot and preheat the oven to 180°C/Gas Mark 4. Remove the lamb from the muslin.

Heat 2 tablespoons of oil in a frying pan. Season the lamb shanks with salt and pepper and sprinkle with the rosemary. Fry the meat until lightly browned all over, about 10 minutes. Remove the meat and replace it with the celery and chopped onion and cook until the onion is transparent. Add the tomato purée and balsamic vinegar and cook until the liquid thickens.

Transfer the mixture to the casserole and add the beef stock, parsley and garlic. Add the meat.

Cover the casserole and bake for 1 hour, then turn the meat and bake for another hour. Serve with mashed potatoes and steamed spinach, or one of Popeye's Spinach Specials.

LOBSCOUSE
WINTER WARMER

This is the classic Liverpool stew, but like all stews it needs slow cooking, for 4 hours at the very least. You can put it in a low oven, go to bed and it will be ready the next morning. Like all stews, it tastes better when reheated. You can also use all lamb, instead of only half lamb. A stewpot is a deep pot or casserole that can be put on the stove or in the oven. When making the stew, as you peel the potatoes drop them in a bowl of cold water, leaving them whole until required.

Serves 8
2 tablespoons wholewheat flour
1 teaspoon salt
1 teaspoon freshly ground black pepper
1 tablespoon olive oil
450 g lean stewing steak, cut into 2 ½ cm cubes
450 g lean lamb, cut into 2 ½ cm cubes
1 large onion, chopped
1 teaspoon Worcester sauce
750 g carrots, scraped and sliced
2 medium turnips, peeled and halved
2.25 kg potatoes, peeled
1 bay leaf
3 sprigs parsley, tied together with string
2 beef stock cubes

Pour the flour into a shallow dish and season with salt and pepper. Heat the oil in a large frying pan. Roll the cubes of meat briefly in the flour and add to the frying pan with the chopped onion. Fry, turning until lightly browned all over. Add the Worcester sauce and cook, stirring occasionally, for another 3 minutes. Transfer the meat and onions to a large stewpot. Add the sliced carrots and the turnips and place them on the meat. Dice 450 g of the potatoes and add them to the carrots. Then add the parsley and bay leaf.

Fill the stewpot with cold water to cover the ingredients until it is half full. Simmer on the stove or in a preheated 180°C/Gas Mark 4 oven for 2 hours.

Slice the remaining potatoes and layer them into the pot with the crumbled beef stock cubes. Simmer for at least another 2 hours. Discard the bay leaf and parsley before serving.

Serve piping hot with red cabbage, cold sliced beetroot, pickled onions and crusty bread.

IRISH STEW
POPEYE'S FAVOURITE FROM THE EMERALD ISLE

This simple stew is easy to make. You can replace the cubed meat with lean lamb chops. You can even add a tin of baked beans to the liquid during the last half hour of cooking.

Serves 6–8
1 kg lamb or mutton, cut into cubes, fat trimmed
salt and pepper
6 tablespoons chopped parsley
1 kg potatoes, peeled and sliced
1 large onion, sliced
2 carrots, sliced
2 x 400 g tinned chopped tomatoes
1 stock cube

Line a lidded casserole with the sliced potatoes, then cover with a layer of meat. Sprinkle with salt and pepper and the parsley. Cover with a layer of sliced onions and a layer of carrots. Repeat the layers until the meat, potatoes, onions and carrots have been used up, ending with a layer of potatoes. Pour the tinned tomatoes and their liquid over the meat.

Bring 600 ml water to the boil. Put the stock cube in a bowl and pour the boiling water over it. Stir until dissolved, then add this liquid to the stew.

Heat the oven to 160°C/Gas Mark 3. Put the lid on the casserole and put the stew in the oven. Cook for 2 hours. Then remove the lid from the casserole, reduce the heat to 150°C/Gas Mark 2 and cook for another 30 minutes to brown the potatoes.

Serve with another cooked vegetable on the side such as cabbage, spinach or green beans.

BEEF OLIVES

These basically consist of pieces of beef filled with vegetables and oven-baked. A lean but inexpensive cut can be used for the beef.

Serves 4
4 x 250 g minute steaks
2 tablespoons oil
2 shallots, chopped
2 garlic cloves, peeled and chopped
3 bacon rashers
100 g flat mushrooms, chopped
2 tablespoons dry breadcrumbs
1 teaspoon dried thyme
2 tablespoons French mustard
1 large onion, coarsely chopped
4 celery sticks, coarsely chopped
3 medium carrots, coarsely chopped
250 ml red wine vinegar
600 ml beef stock

Heat 1 tablespoon of the oil in a frying pan and fry the shallots and garlic until the shallots are translucent. Remove from the pan and then add the bacon. Cook until crisp. Remove from the pan and chop them into small pieces. Replace with the mushrooms. Cook for 1 minute or until they start to soften and give up their juice. In a bowl, combine the shallots, garlic mushrooms, bacon, breadcrumbs and thyme.

Cover a work surface with clingfilm and spread the steaks out flat on it. Place another sheet of clingfilm over the steaks and beat them flat with a steak hammer or heavy rolling pin until they are thinner. Remove the top layer of clingfilm. Spread the steaks evenly with the French mustard.

Divide the stuffing into 4 equal portions. Place 1 portion on each slice of meat, spooning it down the centre of the steak. Roll up each piece of steak into a cylinder. Tie each piece with kitchen string, lengthways and crossways into a parcel.

Heat another tablespoon of the oil in the frying pan and brown the parcels evenly. Transfer them to an oven dish with a lid and reserve. Preheat the oven to 175°C/Gas Mark 4.

Add the rest of the oil to the frying pan and add the coarsely chopped vegetables. Cook them stirring occasionally until the onion is lightly browned. Add the red wine vinegar and stock to the pan and mix well, scraping any residue left in the bottom of the pan. Pour this liquid into the oven dish around the meat. Cover with a lid and bake for 2 ½ hours.

Remove the meat from the oven dish and discard the string. Strain the beef gravy through a sieve. Place the beef olives and gravy in the frying pan and reheat briefly. Serve with mashed potato and a green vegetable.

CHILLI CON CARNE

The chilli powder used in the south-western United States and northern Mexico, where this recipe comes from, is much milder than chilli powder in the UK which is based on an Indian recipe. If you cannot find American or Mexican chilli powder, combine cayenne pepper, sweet paprika and ground cumin in equal quantities.

Serves 8
500 g dried kidney beans, soaked in cold water overnight
1 kg lean stewing beef, cut into cubes, trimmed of fat
2 bay leaves
2 large onions, chopped
3 whole garlic cloves, sliced
2 tablespoons olive oil
1 tablespoon tomato purée
½ teaspoon salt
1 tablespoon cornmeal (or polenta)
½ teaspoon dried sage
½ teaspoon dried oregano
2 tablespoons chilli powder
1 x 400 g tinned tomatoes
1 teaspoon freshly ground black pepper

Drain the beans and place them in a large saucepan with meat. Add enough water to cover and bring to the boil and boil steadily for 10 minutes. Add the bay leaves and sliced garlic cloves.

Cover the pan and simmer on low heat for 2 hours or until the beans are tender. Add olive oil and onions with the tomato purée, salt, cornmeal, sage, oregano and chilli powder and cook for 5 minutes, stirring constantly.

Pour the mixture into the beans and meat, add the tinned tomatoes and cook for a further hour. Season with the pepper just before serving with cornbread and sour cream.

CORNBREAD

No book of American recipes would be complete without cornbread! This is a staple of the Thanksgiving table and eaten at most meals in the South. Like all dishes made with maize, cornbread does not keep: it should be eaten as soon as possible after baking. For a savoury version, omit the sugar and for a spicy version add 2 seeded and chopped jalapeño chilli peppers.

Serves 8
1 egg
125 g sugar
250 g cornmeal (or polenta)
125 g plain flour
½ teaspoon salt
1 teaspoon cream of tartar
½ teaspoon bicarbonate of soda
45 g butter, melted
225 ml milk

Grease a 20 cm by 20 cm baking dish.

Beat the egg in a large bowl or food processor and add the sugar gradually. In another bowl, combine the cornmeal, flour, salt, cream of tartar and bicarbonate of soda. Beat the butter and milk into the dry ingredients and beat in the egg-and-sugar mixture. Make sure the batter is smooth.

Heat the oven to 180°C/Gas Mark 4. Pour the batter into the prepared baking dish and bake for 30 minutes or until a knife blade inserted into the centre comes out clean.

Cut the cornbread into 5 cm squares and serve with jam or honey and yogurt or clotted cream.

CORNED BEEF HASH

This is actually a breakfast dish in the United States, though a rather hearty one, which is why it is Popeye's favourite – especially with a helping of spinach on the side. American corned beef is much saltier than British corned beef, more like salt beef or pastrami, but English corned beef is just as good.

Serves 4
500 g tinned corned beef
2 tablespoons rapeseed oil
1 medium onion, chopped
450 g boiled potatoes, diced
250 ml beef stock
4 eggs
4 tablespoons chopped parsley

Chop the corned beef and put it in a heated non-stick frying pan. When the fat melts, add half the oil, onion and potatoes and cook, stirring, until the potatoes are nicely browned all over, about 10 minutes. Add the beef stock and stir until most of the liquid is absorbed.

Transfer the hash to a serving dish and keep it warm while you fry the eggs in the remaining oil.

To serve, pile some hash on to each plate, top with a fried egg and a sprinkling of parsley.

MEATLOAF SPECIAL

For some reason, meatloaf is an American speciality, although
there is no reason why it shouldn't be enjoyed everywhere. It is a
quick and nutritious main course, but it's also delicious cooled and
chilled with one of Olive Oyl's salads for a picnic.

Serves 6–8
450 g minced beef
250 g minced pork
250 g minced lamb or veal
4 celery sticks, finely chopped
1 small green pepper, seeded and finely chopped
4 tablespoons dried breadcrumbs
4 tablespoons chopped parsley
1 tablespoon dried basil
1 large egg, beaten
1 ½ teaspoons salt
½ teaspoon black pepper
4 hard-boiled eggs
6 rashers streaky bacon
Knob of butter

Preheat the oven to 180°C/Gas Mark 4.

Combine all the ingredients except the bacon and hard-boiled
eggs in a large mixing bowl, or the bowl of a mixer with the hook
attachments. Mix just until combined.

Line a loaf tin with aluminum foil and butter it. Spoon half the
meatloaf mixture into foil. Add the whole shelled eggs in a row
down the centre. Top with the rest of the mixture, shape into a loaf
and cover with the bacon rashers.

Bake for 1 ½ hours. Serve with a savoury sauce, such as mushroom
sauce (page 135) or a rich gravy, mashed potato, and a cooked
vegetable such as cooked spinach.

HEARTY HAMBURGERS

The finest hamburgers are made from meat that has been well hung and that you grind yourself, but if you do not have a food processor suitable for mincing meat (don't use a traditional mincer, it squeezes out too much of the meat juices), then find a friendly butcher to make the leanest mince.

WIMPY'S BBQ HAMBURGER

The secret to Wimpy's hamburgers is that they are not made from beef at all, but from a much leaner animal, the buffalo (American bison). In the UK, use venison. The special sauce and toppings are what make these hamburgers so tasty. When barbecuing, wear an apron and oven gloves.

Serves 8
1 kg lean beef venison steaks, minced
1 teaspoon brown sauce
½ teaspoon hot pepper sauce (optional)
2 eggs, beaten
2 tablespoons olive oil
3 large onions, sliced into rings
4 tablespoons chopped parsley

Mince the venison steaks at home if possible. Combine in a bowl with the brown sauce, hot pepper sauce (if using) and beaten eggs. Shape the meat into hamburger patties. It should make about 16 small patties.

Add the oil to a frying pan and when it is hot add the onion rings. Cook until lightly browned, stirring occasionally, about 10 minutes.

Heat a grill or barbecue to hot. When it is piping hot place the hamburgers on it and cook for 2 to 5 minutes on each side, depending on how well your guests like them done.

When the patties are done, place them on a serving dish and sprinkle with the onion rings and chopped parsley. Serve with the mushroom sauce (page 135) or onion gravy (page 135) and mashed potatoes.

POPEYE'S FAVOURITE HAMBURGER

Popeye's favourite hamburger contains a magic ingredient – beetroot. It's not only delicious, but is a powerful antioxidant!

Serves 4
500 g minced beef
2 medium cooked beetroot, skinned
2 tablespoons wholewheat breadcrumbs
1 large egg, beaten
2 teaspoons cider vinegar
1 teaspoon chopped fresh dill or ½ teaspoon dried dill
1 teaspoon dried parsley
1 tablespoon olive oil
1 small head lettuce, shredded
1 red onion, sliced into rings
250 ml thick-set plain yogurt

Grate the beetroot on a coarse grater and mix it with the beef, breadcrumbs, egg, cider vinegar, dill and parsley. Shape the mixture into 8 burger patties.

Heat the oil in a frying pan and when hot add the burgers. Fry them on each side for 3 minutes if you like them rare in the middle, 5 minutes if you like them cooked through.

While they are cooking, arrange the lettuce on 4 serving plates. Add the cooked burgers and top with the onion rings. Hand the yogurt around separately.

BLUTO'S IRRESISTIBLE HAMBURGER

What makes this hamburger irresistible? The quality of the meat, of course! If you can, buy chuck steak or even rump steak.

The other thing is that Bluto cheats! He adds breadcrumbs and flavourings to his hamburger, then smothers it with a delicious mushroom sauce before he adds the fried onions. You can dispense with hamburger buns and make this irresistible hamburger at home. It goes well with fresh peas and new or mashed potatoes.

Serves 8
1 kg lean minced beef
2 large onions, 1 finely chopped, 1 cut into rings
1 egg, beaten
2 tablespoons dry breadcrumbs
½ teaspoon salt
½ teaspoon freshly ground black pepper
1 tablespoon dried parsley
1 teaspoon dried sage
1 teaspoon onion powder
1 tablespoon olive oil

For the mushroom sauce:
2 large flat mushrooms, including stalks, chopped
2 cloves garlic, peeled and chopped
1 small onion, finely chopped
2 tablespoons finely chopped parsley
1 tablespoon French mustard
2 tablespoons cream cheese or fromage frais
125 ml beef stock

In a bowl, mix the beef, chopped onion, beaten egg, dry breadcrumbs, salt and pepper, dried parsley, dried sage and onion powder in the order given.

With floured hands, shape the meat into hamburger patties. Heat a non-stick frying pan or griddle and cook the hamburgers for 3 minutes on each side. They should be just done in the centre. Reserve in a warm place.

Add the olive oil to the pan juices left by the hamburger and, when hot, cook the onion rings. Drain on paper towels and reserve in a warm place.

To make the mushroom sauce, add the mushrooms, onion and garlic to the hamburger and onion pan and cook until the mushrooms start to give up their juices. Add the parsley, then the mustard and cream cheese or fromage frais, stirring constantly. Add the beef stock and stir until the liquid is smooth.

Arrange the hamburgers on plates or on half a bun. Top with onion rings then pour the mushroom sauce over them. Top with the other half of the bun if using. Otherwise serve with mashed potatoes.

SEVEN VEGETABLE COUSCOUS

This vegetarian couscous is popular in Fez, Morocco. Ras el-hanout is a Moroccan spice mixture, harissa is a Tunisian hot sauce, often sold in tubes like toothpaste. Both are available at big supermarkets. If you cannot find ras el-hanout, use half a teaspoon each of cayenne pepper, ground cumin and ground coriander. If you cannot find harissa, mix a tablespoon of tomato purée with half a teaspoon cayenne pepper.

Serves 6–8
1 small cauliflower, trimmed and divided into florets
1 tablespoon olive oil
1 medium onion, peeled and chopped
2 garlic cloves, peeled and chopped
1 tablespoon ras el-hanout
1 cinnamon stick
1 bay leaf
2 x 400 g tinned chopped tomatoes
1 tablespoon harissa
1 sweet red pepper, seeded and chopped
1 carrot, peeled and sliced
60 g prunes, stoned
450 g pumpkin, peeled and cut into bite-sized chunks
175 g string beans, trimmed, strings removed, sliced
225 g tinned chickpeas
250 g couscous
½ teaspoon salt
freshly ground black pepper

To serve:
harissa mixed with cooking liquid

Soak the cauliflower florets in heavily salted cold water for 20 minutes to get rid of any insects.

Heat the oil in a large frying pan or wok with a lid. Add the onion and garlic and cook until the onion is transparent. Add the ras el-hanout, cinnamon stick, bay leaf, tomatoes, harissa, red pepper, carrot, prunes and pumpkin. Cover and cook for 10 minutes. Then add the cauliflower, chickpeas and beans and cook for another 15 minutes. Add 225 ml water and cover again. Cook for another 10 minutes.

Put the couscous into a bowl and add boiling water to cover. Stir, cover the bowl and leave for 15 minutes or until the water has been absorbed. Season with salt and pepper and fluff the couscous with a fork.

Transfer the couscous to a serving platter and arrange it in a ring around the edge.

Discard the cinnamon stick and bay leaf and mound the vegetable stew in the centre of the serving dish. Serve hot.

Mix a little of the cooking liquid with the extra harissa and pour this hot sauce into a sauceboat. Hand it round separately for those who like their food spicier.

PASTA WITH SPINACH AND RICOTTA

Serves 4
250 g spirali (pasta whirls), preferably multi-coloured
2 tablespoons pine nuts
1 tablespoon olive oil
About 600 g raw spinach leaves, well washed, rinsed and drained
2 garlic cloves, finely chopped
250 g ricotta, cut into cubes
3 tablespoons grated Parmesan cheese, to serve
Salt and pepper

Cook pasta according to directions on the package then drain it. Reserve in a bowl in a warm place.

While the pasta is cooking, add the pine nuts to a large, dry frying pan. Cook, shaking and stirring with a wooden spoon, until the pine nuts start to brown. Remove them from the frying pan and reserve them.

Add the oil to the large frying pan and heat for 1 minute, then add the spinach and garlic. Cook, stirring, until the spinach has wilted, about 7 minutes. Remove it from the pan, drain it, reserving the cooking liquid, and transfer it to a board. When it is cool enough, chop it finely. Stir the ricotta cheese and chopped spinach into the reserved spinach cooking liquid. Season with salt and pepper to taste. Then add the pine nuts and stir well.

Add the spinach mixture to the reserved pasta and stir until well blended. Sprinkle with the Parmesan cheese before serving.
Tip: this can also be made with frozen spinach, which should be put in a saucepan and cooked until hot before you stir the ricotta cheese into it.

Serve with garlic bread and a green salad.

SPAGHETTI AND MEATBALLS

The classic standby: the American equivalent of spaghetti bolognese, for when you can't think of anything else to make. You usually have the ingredients in the store cupboard and fridge – minced meat, tinned tomatoes and spaghetti. I've jazzed it up by including vegetables.

Serves 4
450 g raw minced meat (beef, pork, veal or turkey or a combination)
1 egg, beaten
8 tablespoons chopped parsley
4 tablespoons wholewheat flour
2 tablespoons olive oil
2 onions, finely chopped
2 garlic cloves, peeled and crushed
2 carrots, diced
½ head cabbage, shredded
400 g tinned tomatoes, chopped
200 ml beef stock
2 tablespoons tomato purée
400 g spaghetti
Salt and freshly ground black pepper

Heat 1 tablespoon of the oil in a large, deep frying pan or flameproof casserole over medium heat. Add the onion and garlic and cook for 5 minutes or until the onion is soft. Remove from the heat.

Place the minced meat in a large bowl. Add half the onion and garlic to the meat, then add the beaten egg and half the parsley. Mix well with a fork or with your hands. Shape into balls the size of a walnut then dip them in the flour, tapping to remove excess.

Heat the rest of the oil and fry the meatballs in the remaining onion and garlic, turning them frequently with a wooden spoon, until they are evenly browned. Remove them from the frying pan and reserve them.

Bring a saucepan of water to the boil and add the carrots and cabbage. Boil for 3 minutes then drain and rinse under cold water.

To the large frying pan containing the onion and garlic, add the tinned tomatoes and their juice, stock, tomato purée, carrots and cabbage and bring to the boil, stirring. Reduce the heat, add the meatballs, in a single layer, and simmer gently, stirring occasionally, for 5–6 minutes or until the sauce thickens and the meatballs are heated through.

Meanwhile, bring a large, deep pot of salted water to the boil. Add the spaghetti and boil for about 12 minutes or until al dente. Drain well in a metal colander and rinse under cold water. Reserve in a serving bowl in a warm place while you finish making the sauce.

Add the rest of the parsley to the sauce and stir until well combined. Taste and season with salt and pepper.

Divide the spaghetti between 4 serving bowls and ladle the sauce and meatballs over each portion. Serve immediately.

VEGETABLES

POPEYE'S WITCHES' STEW

Well, this one is certainly tastier than the "eye of newt, and toe of frog" that were some of the ingredients in the stew prepared by the witches in Shakespeare's *Macbeth*! It is even vegetarian. In fact, it looks and tastes suspiciously like a curry!

Serves 4

3 tablespoons sunflower oil
2 medium onions, chopped
2 garlic cloves, peeled and chopped
3 medium potatoes, scrubbed and cut into 2.5 cm cubes
½ medium cauliflower, steeped in salt water for 20 minutes, cut into florets
3 sticks celery, chopped
2 medium courgettes, peeled and sliced
1 large tart apple, peeled, cored and cut into 2.5 cm cubes
2 tablespoons curry powder
2 tablespoons garam masala
4 tablespoons mango chutney
2.5 cm piece of root ginger, peeled and chopped into matchsticks
400 g tinned chopped tomatoes with juice
1 tablespoon yeast extract (e.g. Marmite®)
2 tablespoons besan (chickpea flour/gram flour) (optional)

Heat the oil in a heavy-based saucepan. Add the onions, garlic and diced potatoes and cook until the onion is transparent, about 10 minutes. Add the cauliflower florets and cook for another 5 minutes, stirring occasionally.

Add the celery, courgettes and apple and cook for a further 5 minutes.

Now stir in the curry powder and garam masala and cook, stirring, for 3 minutes. Add the mango chutney, matchsticks of ginger, tomatoes and the yeast extract and continue cooking. Taste and, if the mixture is too spicy or too runny, add the besan. Cook for 10 minutes and serve with long-grain or Basmati rice.

POLISH RED CABBAGE

This winter vegetable dish is a delicious accompaniment to the Thanksgiving or Christmas turkey. Do not cook in aluminium pots as the acidity will cause the aluminium to leach into the food. The recipe calls for vegetable stock to keep this dish vegetarian but you can use meat stock if you are going to serve it with a meat dish.

Serves 8–10
2 medium red cabbages
2 tablespoons coarse salt
450 ml red wine vinegar
4 tablespoons soft brown sugar
125 g sultanas
225 ml vegetable stock
1 tablespoon potato starch

Cut the cabbages in half and discard the tough cores. Shred the cabbages with a sharp knife or with the shredding attachment of a food processor. Put them in a bowl and sprinkle with the salt. Leave for 10 minutes then transfer to a colander, pressing out as much liquid as possible.

Put the cabbages in a stainless steel saucepan and add boiling water just to cover. Bring back to the boil, reduce the heat and simmer until tender. Add the red wine vinegar, brown sugar and sultanas and cook for another 5 minutes.

Combine 2 tablespoons of the stock with the potato starch and stir into the rest of the stock. Pour the liquid into a saucepan and bring to the boil. Add this to the cooked cabbage and stir well to combine. Serve hot.

BUCKWHEAT GROATS WITH WILD MUSHROOMS

The smoky aroma of porcini, the wild mushrooms known in English as ceps or penny bun mushrooms, goes very well with buckwheat groats. The groats, also known as kasha, are a staple of the Russian diet. Porcini are sold dried in supermarkets and delicatessens.

Serves 4–6
125 g dried porcini (ceps)
250 g buckwheat groats (kasha)
1 egg, beaten
½ teaspoon salt
½ teaspoon freshly ground black pepper
1 tablespoon rapeseed oil
500 ml vegetable or chicken stock

Soak the porcini in 250 ml of hot water for 20 minutes. Strain and reserve the mushrooms and liquid.

Pour the buckwheat groats into a bowl and stir the beaten egg into them until each grain is coated. Season with salt and pepper.

Heat the oil in a deep frying pan or wok with a lid and add the groats. Cook, stirring constantly, for 3 minutes or until the grains begin to give off an aroma. Add the soaked mushrooms and their liquid and cook for 5 minutes, stirring occasionally. Add the stock and cover the pan. Reduce the heat and simmer for 10 minutes, then remove the lid, stir the kasha and cook on a low heat for 3–5 minutes until all the liquid has been absorbed.

Serve as a side-dish, or a main course with a green vegetable.

SPINACH AND RICE RING

To make this you will need a 20 cm metal ring mould or other decorative mould.

Serves 4–6
200 g long-grain rice
450 g fresh or frozen spinach
Pinch of ground nutmeg
15 g butter
2 tablespoons green or black olives, stoned and chopped
2 tablespoons shelled pistachio nuts, coarsely chopped
2 tablespoons lemon juice
Freshly ground black pepper
2 bunches watercress, washed, trimmed and chopped
8 cherry tomatoes

Bring a pan of 600 ml water to the boil and add the rice. Cook until al dente, about 15 minutes.

Wash the fresh spinach and trim it. Put it into a saucepan or place the frozen spinach in a saucepan, both without extra water. Add the nutmeg and cook until softened, about 5 minutes.

Place the spinach in a colander and use the back of a wooden spoon to press out as much water as possible. Melt the butter in the saucepan used for the spinach and return the spinach to the pan. Cook gently, stirring continuously, for 1–2 minutes or until reheated.

Mix the spinach with the rice, olives, nuts, lemon juice and pepper. Oil the mould and press the mixture into it. Leave in a warm place for at least 10 minutes before unmoulding. Arrange the chopped watercress in the centre of the ring and add the halved cherry tomatoes.

POMMES ANNA

This delicious potato dish can be served as a side-dish with some of the other recipes or on its own accompanied by extra cheese and some yogurt.

Serves 6
5 large potatoes
3 garlic cloves, chopped
2 spring onions, finely sliced
75 g butter, melted
2 onions, sliced into very thin rings
sea salt and freshly ground black pepper
¼ teaspoon paprika
175 g Cheddar cheese, finely grated

Peel the potatoes and slice them into thin rounds (about 3 mm thick). Soak them in iced water for at least 30 minutes. Drain and pat dry with kitchen towels.

Add the garlic and spring onions to the melted butter. Heat the oven to 200°C/Gas Mark 6.

Butter a deep ovenproof dish, preferably one you can bring to the table. Arrange one third of the potato slices in the bottom, slightly overlapping, beginning with a ring of slices around the outside and moving into the middle.

Cover the potatoes with one third of the onion rings, then coat with one third of the butter mixture. Season with salt and pepper, a little of the paprika and one third of the cheese. Add another layer of potatoes and another layer of onion rings, butter mixture, seasoning and cheese. Do this once more, ending with a layer of cheese.

Cover the dish with foil and bake for 45 minutes. Remove the foil and bake for 15 minutes or until the cheese topping is browned and bubbling.

PERSIAN SPINACH RICE

Did you know that the very word "spinach" comes from the Persian "esfenaj"? The fact that the Persians are particularly fond of spinach and use it a lot in their cooking makes their cookery a favourite with Popeye! This is a vegetarian dish. It can be served with any kind of meat, if desired, especially lamb, chicken or duck. You can also cook the rice in a rice steamer if you have one.

Serves 4
225 g long-grain or Basmati rice, soaked in salted water for 1 hour
2 tablespoons olive oil
450 g fresh spinach, washed, trimmed and coarsely chopped
1 large onion, finely chopped
½ teaspoon saffron strands
½ teaspoon ground cinnamon
½ teaspoon ground cloves
¼ teaspoon ground nutmeg
225 ml chicken or vegetable stock
225 ml orange juice, unsweetened
1 tablespoon lime juice
50 g sultanas
Sea salt and freshly ground black pepper
2 tablespoons blanched, slivered almonds
1 tablespoon shelled pistachio nuts
2 tablespoons finely chopped flat-leaved parsley

First, place the saffron strands in a little water to soak. Place the soaked rice in a deep pot with a tight-fitting lid and add 1 tablespoon of the oil and 750 ml water. Cover the pot with a cloth or piece of muslin, then add the lid. Bring to the boil , add the softened saffron and cook on a low heat for 20 minutes, checking once to ensure the rice does not burn. Remove from the heat and reserve in a warm place.

Heat the remaining oil in a deep non-stick frying pan with a lid and cook the onion until transparent. Add the saffron rice, cinnamon, cloves and nutmeg and cook, sitrring occasionally, for five minutes. Add the stock, orange juice, sultanas and lime juice. Bring to the boil, cover and reduce the heat. Cook on a low heat until the liquid has been absorbed.

Place the spinach in a pan and add 250 ml water. Cover the pan and cook for 3 minutes or until the spinach wilts. Drain the spinach in a colander, pressing it down with the back of a spoon to remove excess liquid. Leave to stand, covered, while you toast the almonds.

Place the almonds in a dry non-stick frying pan and toast them over a medium heat, stirring and shaking the pan to ensure they brown evenly. When cooked, mix them with the pistachio nuts.

Transfer the rice mixture to the centre of a warmed serving dish. Ladle the spinach mixture round it. Scatter the nut mixture over it, then sprinkle with the parsley. Serve immediately.

HOPPIN' JOHN

No one knows how this dish got its name. All that is certain is that it is a classic Southern accompaniment to a main course. The "black-eyed peas" (which are actually beans) have a number of other names and only grow in the American South. Carolina rice is neither long nor short grain so any kind of rice can be used, including Italian rice. Never add salt to beans before they are cooked. For a vegetarian version, omit the bacon and sprinkle with vegetarian bacon-flavoured "bits" made from soy or textured vegetable protein before serving.

Serves 4
250 g black-eyed peas, soaked in cold water overnight
3 rashers streaky bacon, rind removed
1 onion, chopped
2 garlic cloves, peeled and crushed
½ teaspoon hot pepper sauce
½ teaspoon dried thyme
125 g Carolina or other rice
Extra water or vegetable stock if necessary

Drain the beans and transfer them to a saucepan. Cover with water and bring to the boil. Simmer for 30 minutes or until tender.

Fry the bacon rashers in a non-stick frying pan until crispy. Remove them from the pan and chop them into little pieces. Replace the bacon with the onion and garlic, and fry until the onion is transparent.

Add the onion, garlic, bacon, hot pepper sauce, thyme and rice to the peas and simmer for 15 minutes. If the liquid has dried out, add more water or stock, but the dish should be dry when ready.

GREEN TOMATO PIE

In New Mexico, this pie is made either with genuine green tomatoes, or with tomatillos, which look like tomatoes but are in fact members of the same family as physalis, also known as the Cape gooseberry or Peruvian cherry. It is an excellent way of using up unripe tomatoes from your greenhouse.

Serves 8
For the green tomato filling:
8 green tomatoes, sliced as thinly as possible
25 g butter, cut into small pieces
225 g soft brown sugar
1 tablespoon golden syrup
½ teaspoon ground allspice
½ teaspoon ground cinnamon
125 ml cider vinegar
1 tablespoon potato flour

For the pie dough:
250 g plain flour
½ teaspoon salt
125 g butter, chilled
45 g lard, chilled
1 egg mixed with 1 tablespoon water, to glaze

Butter a 22.5 cm pie dish and cover the base with non-stick baking paper.

Make the savoury dough following the instructions on page 141 and refrigerate for at least 30 minutes.

Remove from the refrigerator and divide the dough into two pieces. Roll out one piece on a floured work surface into a round and cover the bottom and sides of the dish. Dot the bottom of the dish with half the butter and arrange a layer of overlapping tomato slices in the bottom of the dish.

Combine the sugar, golden syrup, allspice, cinnamon and cider vinegar. Sprinkle some of the mixture over the tomato layer, then sprinkle with a little of the potato flour. Cover with another layer of tomatoes and more of the sugar mixture and potato flour. Top with a third layer of tomatoes and sprinkle with the rest of the sugar mixture. Continue until all these ingredients are used up.

Preheat the oven to 220°C/Gas Mark 7.

Roll out the rest of the dough and use it to cover the pie. Cut a cross in the centre and fold back the flaps of dough so there is a hole through which the steam can escape. Brush the crust with the egg glaze.

Bake the pie for 30 minutes, then reduce the heat to 190°C/Gas Mark 5 and continue baking for 40 minutes. Serve with Cheddar cheese for a savoury lunch or vanilla ice cream for an unusual dessert.

SWEE'PEA'S SWEETS

GRAN'MA'S APPLE PIE

Pastry-making looks hard but it really isn't. The thing to remember is to keep all the ingredients as cold as possible and touch them as little as possible. That is why it is better to make pastry in a food processor than by hand. Rolling it out on a work surface on which you have placed non-stick baking paper is a foolproof way of transferring the rolled out dough to the pie dish!

Makes a 22 cm apple pie

For the pastry:
275 g plain flour
1 teaspoon salt
75 g cold butter
75 g cold lard (or vegetable shortening)
1 tablespoon sugar
1 egg, beaten
2 ½ tablespoons water

For the topping:
1 egg yolk, beaten with 2 tablespoons water

For the filling:
125 g unsalted butter
3 tablespoons plain flour
4 tablespoons water
125 g demerara sugar
125 g muscovado sugar
1 teaspoon ground cinnamon
½ teaspoon ground allspice
8 Granny Smith apples, peeled, cored and sliced

To make the pie dough, sift the flour and salt into the bowl of a food processor. Cut the lard and butter into pieces and add them. Process until the mixture resembles breadcrumbs. Gradually add the sugar, egg and water until the dough is smooth (it may require a tablespoon or two more water if it is very dry, this depends on the flour). Take the dough out of the processor, wrap it in clingfilm and then chill in the refrigerator for at least 1 hour.

To make the filling, melt the butter in a saucepan. Stir in flour to form a paste. Add water, sugars, cinnamon and allspice and bring to a boil. Reduce temperature and simmer for 5 minutes. Remove from the heat.

Preheat the oven to 220°C/Gas Mark 7.

Spread sheets of non-stick baking paper on a work surface and sprinkle them with flour. Roll out the dough on the non-stick baking paper to a thickness of about 5 mm. Cut a 22 cm diameter circle (or whatever size will fit the pan) out of the dough. Gather up the scraps of dough and roll the dough out again to make the pie lid.

Transfer the bottom crust by carrying it on a sheet of non-stick baking paper and turning it upside down into the tin. Arrange the apples on top and pour the sugar and butter mixture over them. The pie lid can either be a whole piece of dough or you can make a lattice pattern by cutting long strips of dough into 3 cm wide strips and laying them in both directions across the pie.

Bake the pie for 15 minutes then reduce the temperature to 180°C/ Gas Mark 4. Continue baking for 40 minutes. Remove the pie from the oven and brush with the egg yolk mixture. Return to the oven and bake for another 5 minutes. Serve hot or cold, with ice cream or low-fat crème fraîche.

YORKSHIRE PARKIN

Parkin is a gingerbread made with oats and is especially popular in the United Kingdom on Bonfire Night, November 5th, celebrating the famous failure of Yorkshireman Guy Fawkes to blow up the Houses of Parliament in 1605. This Parkin recipe is easy to make and creates a moist, sticky cake. Because the cake must be stored before eating, you should make it well in advance.

Serves 12
125 g butter, softened
125 g soft dark brown sugar
55 g black treacle (black strap molasses)
200 g golden syrup
250 g medium porridge oats
55 g wholewheat flour, sifted
55 g rye flour, sifted
2 teaspoons baking powder, sifted
2 teaspoons ground ginger
2 teaspoons ground allspice
1 teaspoon ground nutmeg
2 medium eggs, beaten
1 tablespoon milk
1 egg yolk, mixed with 2 teaspoons water
12 almonds, blanched and split in half

Line a 20 cm by 20 cm square cake tin with non-stick baking paper. In a large heavy-based saucepan over a gentle heat melt the butter and add the sugar, treacle and golden syrup. Stir until combined, then remove from the heat without allowing the mixture to get too hot.

In a large bowl, combine the oats, flours, baking powder and the spices. Gradually beat in the melted butter-and-treacle mixture until all the ingredients are combined.

Preheat the oven to 140°C/Gas Mark 1.

Add the beaten eggs and mix thoroughly. Finally add the milk and mix again. Pour the mixture into the prepared tin. Brush the surface with the egg yolk to glaze it, then add the almonds, pressing them into the surface lightly in an even pattern. Bake for 1 ½ hours or until a knife blade inserted in the centre comes out clean.

Remove from the oven and leave to cool in the tin. Store the Parkin in an airtight tin for a minimum of 3 days and up to a week before eating; this allows the flavours to develop and the mixture to soften and become moist and sticky.

MELTING CHOCOLATE PUDDING

EVERYBODY'S SUNDAY FAVOURITE

Serves 6
150 g self-raising flour
4 tablespoons cocoa powder
50 g ground almonds
100 g dark chocolate (70% cocoa mass), roughly chopped
200 g castor sugar
175 ml milk
50 g butter, melted
1 egg

For the chocolate sauce:
150 g dark muscovado sugar
3 tablespoons cocoa powder
300 ml boiling water

To make the chocolate sponge pudding, heat the oven to 180°C/ Gas Mark 4. Mix the flour, cocoa powder, ground almonds, chocolate and sugar together. Then stir the milk, butter and egg together and mix into the dry ingredients. Spoon into 6 individual ramekins or ovenproof dishes.

To make the sauce, mix the sugar and cocoa powder and gradually stir in 300 ml boiling water. Spoon this over the sponge mixture. Bake the puddings for 20 minutes. Lower the oven temperature to 150°C/Gas Mark 2 and cook for a further 10 minutes until the sponge feels firm to the touch – the sauce will be lurking underneath. Serve straight from the oven with cream.

CHERRY CLAFOUTIS
A DESSERT POPEYE FOUND IN FRANCE

This lovely cherry dessert is one of Popeye's favourites, but don't make it with canned cherries, use only fresh or frozen. It is fun to make because you put the cherries in the bottom of the pan and they rise to the surface during baking. You can buy cherry-stoners but it is just as easy to cut the cherries in half and stone them (messy though!). You can use powdered sweetener or high-sweetened sugar instead of sugar, but reduce the quantity to half (75 g).

Serves 8
125 g blanched almonds
500 g fresh or frozen morello cherries, stoned
150 g sugar
1 teaspoon cornflour
½ teaspoon ground cinnamon
75 ml all-purpose flour
4 large eggs
½ teaspoon salt
250 ml semi-skimmed milk
50 g unsalted butter
1 teaspoon grated lemon rind
1 teaspoon vanilla essence
½ teaspoon almond essence
2 tablespoons icing sugar

Butter or oil a square glass or ceramic baking dish. Toast the almonds in a dry non-stick frying pan.

In a bowl, combine the cherries with 1 tablespoon of sugar, the cornflour and the cinnamon. Pour the mixture into the prepared baking dish.

In a food processor, combine the flour and toasted almonds until the almonds are finely chopped.

Preheat the oven to 220°C/Gas Mark 7.

In a large bowl, beat the eggs with the salt and the rest of the sugar. Gradually beat in the flour-and-nut mixture. Add the milk, butter, lemon rind and vanilla and almond essences and beat until smooth. Pour this mixture over the cherries in the baking dish. Bake the clafoutis for 25 minutes.

Remove from the oven and cool for 5 minutes before sprinkling it with icing sugar. Serve immediately with low-fat crème fraîche.

MISSISSIPPI MUD PIE

This pie is unbaked and uses a chocolate bourbon crust. It is very chocolatey and so very sugary, but let's remember that chocolate is supposed to be good for you! The pie is named after the thick, dark mud of the Mississippi Delta. The Chocolate Fudge Topping can be made in advance and used to top vanilla ice cream to make a Chocolate Fudge Sundae.

Serves 8–10
280 g chocolate Bourbon biscuits
125 g butter, melted
½ ground mixed spice
1 litre vanilla ice cream, softened
2 tablespoons instant coffee
3 tablespoons cocoa powder

For the Chocolate Fudge Topping:
50 g butter
75 ml low-fat cream
2 tablespoons cocoa powder
110 g muscovado sugar
175 ml golden syrup
1 teaspoon vanilla essence
Mini marshmallows and chocolate sprinkles to garnish

Crush the chocolate biscuits into fine crumbs by putting them in a plastic bag and rolling them with a rolling pin. Pour the melted butter into a bowl, then add the crushed biscuits and mixed spice, and mix well. Press this mixture into a 23 cm pie dish or flan tin. Refrigerate until required.

Place the softened ice cream in a bowl and beat in the cocoa powder and instant coffee, beating until smooth. Spoon the ice cream into the pie crust and place in the freezer for at least 8 hours. To make the Chocolate Fudge Topping, melt the butter in a saucepan and add the rest of the ingredients. Heat, stirring constantly with a wooden spoon. Bring to the boil and boil for 5 minutes. Remove from the heat, leave to cool, then refrigerate until required.

When ready to serve, pour the Chocolate Fudge Topping over the pie, and decorate with mini marshmallows and chocolate sprinkles.

SHOOFLY PIE

This sticky treacle pie is traditional among the so-called Pennsylvania Dutch or Amish, the German and Swiss religious Protestants who emigrated to Pennsylvania, a state in which freedom of religion was strictly upheld, in the 17th and 18th centuries. There are several versions; this is the one known as "wet bottom".

Serves 8
For the pie dough:
200 g plain wholewheat flour
2 tablespoons icing sugar
75 g cold butter, cut into pieces
1 egg yolk
Iced water

For the topping:
100 g wholewheat flour
100 g muscovado sugar
½ teaspoon mixed spice
½ teaspoon ground ginger
½ teaspoon ground cinnamon
50 g cold butter, cut into pieces

For the filling:
2 eggs
125 ml black treacle (black strap molasses)
½ teaspoon bicarbonate of soda
4 tablespoons demerara sugar

To make the pie dough, follow the instructions on page 141. Flour a work surface. Knead the dough lightly on the work surface and roll it out to fit a 23 cm fluted, loose-bottomed flan tin. Refrigerate until required.

To make the topping, sift the flour, sugar and spices into a bowl. Add the butter and mix until the mixture resembles breadcrumbs. Spoon one-third of the mixture into the pastry case.

Preheat the oven to 190°C/Gas Mark 5.

To make the filling, use a hand-held whisk to beat the eggs with the treacle. Put the bicarbonate of soda into a small bowl. Boil 125 ml water and pour it over the bicarbonate which will foam. Immediately pour this into the treacle-and-egg mixture and beat well.

Pour this into the pastry case and cover with the rest of the topping mixture, spreading it as evenly as possible with a plastic spatula. Sprinkle with the demerara sugar.

Bake the pie for 35 minutes. Serve with vanilla ice cream.

GOOSEBERRY CRUMBLE

Crumble toppings are so quick and easy, and turn plain stewed fruit into something special. You can use jumbo oats, rolled oats or even muesli for the topping.

Serves 4
500 g gooseberries, "topped and tailed"
1 lemon, rind grated, juice squeezed
3 tablespoons castor sugar (or to taste)
1 tablespoon cornflour
130 g raw oats
4 tablespoons soft brown sugar
½ teaspoon cinnamon
½ teaspoon nutmeg
50 g butter, cut into pieces

Place the gooseberries in water to cover, and cook, uncovered, with the lemon juice and rind on low heat until soft, about 10 minutes.

Drain the gooseberries and stir the castor sugar into the juice. Then stir in the cornflour and return to the boil. Cook, stirring, until thickened. Remove from the heat and return the reserved gooseberries to the liquid.

Combine the oats with the brown sugar, cinnamon and nutmeg. Heat the oven to 180°C/Gas Mark 4.

Pour the stewed fruit into a soufflé baking dish and sprinkle with the topping. Dot it with the pieces of butter. Bake for 30 minutes and serve hot or cold.

INDIVIDUAL ORANGE SOUFFLÉS

Serves 8
8 large navel oranges
25 g butter
175 g sugar
4 tablespoons self-raising flour
2 oranges, rind grated
2 eggs, separated
225 ml semi-skimmed milk
¼ teaspoon salt
8 fresh mint sprigs for decoration

Cut the tops off the oranges neatly, about one-third of the way down, and scoop out the contents, keeping the orange skins whole. Strain the juice from the oranges. Cream the butter and sugar, beating them together until smooth, and add the flour, 125 ml orange juice (reserve the rest of the orange juice for another dish) and the finely grated orange rind. Beat the egg yolks with the milk and salt. Fold this mixture into the butter-and-sugar mixture. With an egg-beater, whisk the whites into very stiff peaks and fold them into the mixture using a metal spoon.

Preheat the oven to 200°C/Gas Mark 6.

Fill the scooped out oranges with the mixture. Half-fill a roasting tin with very hot, but not boiling, water, and stand the filled orange cases (you may need to cut a sliver off the bottom of each orange to make it stand up, but be careful not to cut right through). Bake for 10 minutes then reduce the heat to 180°C/Gas Mark 4 and cook for another 20 minutes or until lightly browned on top.

Decorate with fresh mint sprigs and serve immediately.

STRAWBERRY SHORTCAKES

This Southern favourite is perfect for the couple of months when English strawberries are at their best, but at other times of the year you could replace them with raspberries or blackberries.

Serves 8
225 g plain flour
1 tablespoon castor sugar
Pinch of salt
1 tablespoon baking powder
125 g butter, cut into pieces
150 ml milk
2 small eggs, beaten separately
300 g strawberries, washed, hulled and sliced in half

To serve:
Low-fat strawberry-flavoured topping (see below)
A sprig of mint

Sift the flour, baking powder, sugar and salt into a bowl. Rub the butter into the flour until the mixture looks like breadcrumbs. Add the milk and 1 of the eggs and knead to a soft dough.

On a floured work surface, roll out the dough until it is 1 cm thick. Use a fluted biscuit cutter to cut it into 8 cm x 5 cm rounds. Preheat the oven to 220°C/Gas Mark 7.

Cover a baking sheet with non-stick baking paper and place the rounds on the sheet. Brush them with the other egg. Bake for 15 minutes or until golden brown.

Remove from the oven and, while still warm, split the shortcakes in half. Prepare the topping (as below) and place a dollop on the bottom half of each shortcake. Cover with sliced strawberries and cover with the other half of the shortcake. Top with 2 strawberry halves and a mint sprig. Serve immediately.

LOW-FAT STRAWBERRY TOPPING

To make 8 portions
125 g strawberries, fresh or frozen
125 ml low-fat crème fraîche or half-fat cream
1 tablespoon castor sugar or 2 tablespoons of runny honey

Hull the strawberries and wash them well. Thaw them if frozen and slice them in half.

Put all but 8 halves in a bowl and mash them, then mix them with the crème fraîche. Fold in the sugar or honey and use a stick blender or a food processor to blend the mixture until smooth. Decorate with the strawberry halves.

PEACH COBBLER

Peach cobbler is a classic American dessert, especially in Georgia, a state famous for its peaches. It is a sort of peach pie without a base, but instead of pastry the peaches are covered with scones resembling cobblestones. Always use fresh fruits (you can also use nectarines). If you are using the small, flat, white-fleshed clingstone peaches you will need to double the quantity. Experiment with different flavours of yogurt for the topping.

Serves 8
8 large ripe peaches
½ lemon, juice squeezed
2 tablespoons self-raising flour
2 tablespoons soft brown sugar
1 teaspoon cinnamon
2 tablespoons peach or apricot jam or honey
25 g butter, cut into pieces

For the topping:
200 g self-raising flour
1 tablespoon sugar
50 g butter, cold, cut into pieces
1 egg
125 ml plain or flavoured yogurt

Butter a 20 cm round cake tin or Pyrex® dish. Slice the peaches and sprinkle them with the lemon juice. Arrange them neatly in the cake tin.

Combine the flour, brown sugar and cinnamon and sprinkle the mixture over the fruit. Warm the jam or honey until it is of pouring consistency, then pour it over the flour mixture.

To make the topping in a food processor, sift the flour with the sugar and then add the pieces of butter until the mixture resembles breadcrumbs. Beat the egg with the yogurt and combine this with the flour mixture just until you have a smooth dough – do not overmix.

Preheat the oven to 220°C/Gas Mark 7.

Divide the dough into 8 rounds and arrange them over the fruit. Bake for 30 minutes. Serve with a sauce made of warmed peach, apricot or raspberry jam.

FOURTH OF JULY LEMON MERINGUE PIE

In Southern California, Popeye's home territory, both American Independence Day and Thanksgiving Day are celebrated with this pie, because the idea is to use local, easily available ingredients, and lemons and fresh eggs are certainly plentiful in California. Most Californians with a garden have a lemon tree right in their backyard. Americans love a really high, fluffy meringue so if you have any egg whites left over from another recipe, add them when making the meringue. Glucose syrup is available from chemists and good supermarkets. It is used in confectionery to prevent syrups from crystallising.

Serves 8
For the pastry:
250 g plain flour
½ teaspoon salt
1 teaspoon lemon juice
1 teaspoon castor sugar
1 egg yolk
75 g cold butter, cut into pieces (plus extra for greasing the pie dish)

For the filling:
2 lemons, rind grated, juice squeezed and strained
5 egg yolks
2 tablespoons potato flour or thickener
250 ml water

For the meringue:
1 tablespoon corn or glucose syrup
4 tablespoons castor sugar
5 egg whites
60 ml water

Make a special pastry dough for the lemon meringue pie, using the ingredient quantities above and following the instructions for making a sweet pastry on page 141.

Preheat the oven to 200°C/Gas Mark 6. Butter a 22.5 cm circular pie dish. On a floured work surface, roll out the dough into a circle to fit the pie dish. Trim the edges and transfer the dough, wrapped round a rolling pin, to the pie dish. Cut out a circle of non-stick baking paper to fit the bottom of the pie. Place it over the pastry and weigh it down with baking beans. Bake the pie for 15 minutes. Remove it from the oven, discard the non-stick baking paper and beans and return it to the oven for 5–10 minutes or until golden.

While the pie is baking, make the lemon filling. Combine the potato flour or thickener with the lemon juice and 125 ml water. Stir well until smooth then add 125 ml water with the egg yolks and the lemon juice and rind. Transfer to a saucepan and bring to the boil, stirring to prevent lumps from forming.

Pour the lemon filling slowly into the pie crust, making sure that it touches the crust all the way round and ensuring there are no bubbles. Reduce the oven temperature to 180°C/Gas Mark 4.

To make the meringues, heat the sugar with the 60 ml of water and add the corn or glucose syrup. Do not let crystals form on the sides of the pan: brush them away with a wet pastry brush. Cook the syrup for 2 minutes. Whip the egg whites into soft peaks, using an egg whisk or hand-held blender. Then pour the syrup in a steady stream into the egg whites, beating constantly until the mixture is firm. Pile the meringue on top of the pie and bake until it just begins to colour, about 15 minutes.

PLUM DUFF

Plum Duff is a pudding made from plums but the term "plum pudding" is usually used for Christmas Pudding, which contains no plums! Since "plum" is also an old word applied to raisins, Plum Duff is the real pudding. It is popular in the UK and the USA, but the American version is baked whereas the British version is usually steamed and uses chopped fruit.

Serves 6–8
500 g large fresh plums, halved and stoned
1 lemon, rind grated, juice squeezed
125 g self-raising flour, sifted
220 g dried fruit (currants or sultanas)
125 g ground almonds
125 g dark brown sugar
½ teaspoon mixed spice
½ teaspoon ground cinnamon
½ teaspoon grated nutmeg
¼ teaspoon almond essence
2 eggs, beaten
About 250 ml milk

Butter a flameproof casserole or Pyrex® dish of the right size to hold the plums tightly and arrange them, cut side upward, in one layer in the dish. Sprinkle with the lemon juice. Combine the sifted flour with the lemon rind, ground almonds, dark brown sugar, spices, almond essence and eggs and mix together well. Begin adding the milk gradually and stir well. Keep adding milk just until the mixture drops easily from the spoon when lifted from the bowl. Spoon the mixture over the plums.

Preheat the oven to 180°C/Gas Mark 4. Bake the pudding for 30 minutes or until the topping has risen and is lightly browned on top.

SWEE'PEA'S CHEESECAKE

The special thing about this cheesecake is the crust. Instead of boring old digestive biscuits, this crust uses crushed ginger snaps, which contrast nicely with the cool, fragrant flavour of the filling. This is an unbaked cheesecake.

Serves 10–12
25 g unsalted butter
75 g thin ginger snaps, crushed with a rolling pin
2 tablespoons castor sugar
3 limes, rind grated, juice squeezed
1 tablespoon powdered gelatine
350 g quark or low-fat fromage frais
200 ml thick-set low-fat natural yoghurt
6 tablespoons powdered low-fat milk
Fresh berries or lemon zest

Line the base of a 25 cm springform cake tin with a circle of non-stick baking paper, cut to fit, and butter it and the sides of the tin.

Make the cheesecake base by melting the butter and stirring in the ginger snaps. Spread the mixture over the cake tin base, pressing down well with the back of a wooden spoon. Refrigerate while you make the filling.

To make the filling, pour 125 ml water into a saucepan and sprinkle the powdered gelatine on top. Leave for 5 minutes and then place on the heat. Stir until the gelatine has dissolved into the water, but do not allow to boil. Remove from the heat and set aside.

In a bowl, combine the quark or fromage frais with the yogurt, powdered milk and sugar. Beat with electric beaters or a hand-held blender until smooth. Add the grated lime rind, lime juice and dissolved gelatine and beat again until smooth.

Remove the cake tin from the refrigerator and pour the filling mixture carefully into it. Place it on a plate in case any of the filling leaks out and return it to the refrigerator. Chill for at least 5 hours or overnight.

When ready to serve, garnish with fresh berries or strips of lemon zest.

SUPER PARTY TRIFLE

There are as many recipes for trifle as there are days in the year; whole books have been written about nothing else! All that is definite about trifle is that it consists of sponge cake, custard, and usually masses of whipped cream, jelly and fruit. There is usually a heavy dose of alcohol, such as sherry or liqueurs, which is why one version of trifle is known as Tipsy Cake. This is a simple basic recipe which you can vary as you please. When strawberries are out of season, use fresh sliced peaches or nectarines. If you can't find mini marshmallows cut large ones into 4 pieces each.

Serves 8
250 ml strawberry jelly (preferably sugarless)
500 g sponge cake, cut into 2.5 cm cubes
125 ml sweet wine or sherry
250 ml strawberry yogurt
175 ml vanilla yogurt
250 ml canned or instant custard
75 g fresh strawberries, sliced
1 tablespoon flaked coconut
Mini marshmallows
Hundreds-and-thousands

Make the jelly the day before.

Place cake cubes in a large glass bowl. Sprinkle with the sherry. Chop up the jelly and arrange it on top.

Combine the two yogurts and spoon them over the jelly. Top with half the strawberries and then add the custard. Sprinkle with coconut, marshmallows, remaining strawberries and finally the hundreds-and-thousands.

KEY LIME PIE

This is a low-fat version of Florida's answer to California's Lemon Meringue Pie. The hot, humid Florida climate is ideal for growing limes, which are more tropical than most other citrus fruits. Of course, you can also use the Lemon Meringue Pie recipe (page 115) and substitute 8 very fresh limes for the lemons. To crush biscuits evenly, put them in a plastic bag and crush them with a rolling pin. You will need a lemon zester.

Serves 8
375 g digestive biscuits or ginger snaps, crushed
1 tablespoon potato starch
3 tablespoons castor sugar
25 g butter
8 limes, rind of 7 grated, juice squeezed
375 ml thick-set plain yogurt
125 g low-fat curd cheese
5 drops homemade green food colouring (page 140)
Silver balls

Combine the biscuit crumbs and the butter in a small saucepan. Using a spatula or the back of a spoon, press the mixture into the base of a 23 cm loose-bottomed fluted flan tin. Refrigerate for at least 1 hour.

Heat the potato starch with 125 ml water and stir until the mixture thickens. Allow to cool slightly then pour into a bowl. Add the lime juice and zest of 7 of the limes and add the yogurt, cheese, sugar and the green colouring. Whisk for 1–2 minutes. Pour filling on to the biscuit base. Refrigerate for 2 hours or overnight.

To serve, remove thin strips from the reserved lime with the lemon zester and use them and the silver balls to decorate the pie.

COTTAGE CHEESE PANCAKES WITH CHOCOLATE SAUCE

Makes 8 pancakes (2 per serving)
For the batter:
8 tablespoons strong plain flour
½ teaspoon salt
4 eggs
500 ml semi-skimmed milk
olive oil for frying
(See page 13 for method)

Add to the batter as you beat it:
1 teaspoon castor sugar
1 teaspoon ground cinnamon

For the filling:
500 g cottage cheese at room temperature
1 teaspoon castor sugar (use honey if you prefer)
1 teaspoon cinnamon

Use the method to make the batter for Popeye's Pancakes on page 13.

For the filling, beat the cottage cheese, sugar and cinnamon in a bowl using a wooden spoon. As the pancakes come out of the pan, place them flat and spread a tablespoon of the filling over each. Roll up the pancakes and leave them on a plate in a warm place.

For the chocolate sauce:
1 bar (250 g) baking milk chocolate
125 ml warm milk

Heat the milk in a saucepan. Break the chocolate into pieces and put it in a plastic bowl. Place the bowl in a microwave oven on its lowest setting. Microwave the chocolate for 2 minutes or as per the manufacturer's instructions.

Remove it from the microwave oven and mix with the milk. Pour the sauce into a sauceboat or place 2 pancakes on a plate and pour a ribbon of chocolate sauce over them. Serve immediately.

SWEET POTATO PONE
"I Y'AM WHAT I Y'AM!"™

This favourite dish in the Deep South and the Caribbean is made with yellow-fleshed sweet potatoes known in the southern and south-western American states as "yams". They are related to Morning Glory and have very pretty leaves and flowers, if you choose to grow one as a houseplant. They are no relation at all to the familiar potato. Raw sweet potatoes are harder to peel than the familiar potato because their flesh is denser, but the skin comes away from the flesh when cooked, so it is easiest to peel them when they have first been parboiled or baked.

Serves 4–6
4 medium yellow-fleshed sweet potatoes, washed
4 medium carrots, scraped and washed
200 g prunes (buy already stoned prunes)
2 tablespoons runny honey
1 teaspoon allspice
½ teaspoon grated nutmeg
25 g butter
2 tablespoons demerara sugar
Pinch of salt

Bring a saucepan of salted water to the boil and boil the sweet potatoes and carrots until tender, about 20 minutes. Drain and cool. Peel the sweet potatoes and cut away any inedible parts of the carrots.

Cook the prunes in water to cover for 15 minutes. Remove from the heat and reserve the cooking liquid. Stone the prunes, if necessary, and chop them.

Transfer the potatoes and carrots to a food processor and add the honey, allspice, nutmeg and 250 ml of the prune cooking liquid. Process until smooth. Stir in the chopped prunes.

Butter a square baking dish. Preheat the oven to 190°C/Gas Mark 5. Transfer the mixture to the baking dish, smooth the surface and sprinkle it with the demerara sugar.

Bake the pone for 20 minutes or until lightly browned on top. Serve immediately with crème fraîche or thick-set yogurt.

BOOKMAKER'S SANDWICHES

This is just a funny name for the steak sandwich, once a favourite at the racetrack as it was a meal in itself. These miniature versions make a tasty party snack.

Makes 6 miniature sandwiches
175 g fillet steak, all fat trimmed away
Salt and pepper
3 tablespoons horseradish sauce
1 tablespoon French mustard
2 bread crusts cut from the end of a sandwich loaf, buttered
6 sprigs lamb's lettuce (mâche) or other salad leaf
3 baby radishes

Grill or fry the steak on both sides between 4 and 7 minutes, depending on preference. Season with salt and pepper. Combine the horseradish sauce and mustard and spread them over the steak.

Place the steak between the 2 buttered crusts. It should not protrude over the edges, if it does, trim it back. Tie securely with string to prevent the filling escaping. Wrap the sandwich in 3 sheets of kitchen towel and place it under a heavy weight, such as a plate with 2 heavy tins of food on top. Leave for 30 minutes.

Unwrap the sandwich and cut it into 6 squares. The meat juices will have saturated the bread. Top with the lamb's lettuce and a slice of radish.

TREACLE TOFFEE

Toffee is easy to make, but the toffee has to be boiled to a very high temperature, which can be dangerous, so it is always best to have someone else to help you. Always use a pan with a heavy base or the toffee will burn. You will also need a sugar thermometer as the toffee must boil to exactly the right temperature.

You can make the toffee well before you need it. It keeps very well.

Makes 500 g toffee
450 g muscovado sugar
125 ml water
¼ teaspoon cream of tartar
125 g black treacle
125 ml golden syrup

Thickly butter a 30 cm x 10 cm or 18 cm square tin.

In a large heavy-based saucepan, dissolve the sugar and water. Add the rest of the ingredients, increase the heat and bring to the boil. Boil to 140°C (the soft crack stage), testing with a sugar thermometer. This should take about 10 minutes.

Remove the pan from the heat and hold the base under cold running water to stop the cooking process. Pour the toffee into the tin. When it has cooled and started to solidify, score it with a knife into squares. Leave it to cool completely.

Once the toffee is cold, remove it from the tin and break it with a steak mallet, or other small hammer: the toffee will crack into pieces. Wrap it in non-stick baking paper and store in an airtight tin.

PEACH-FLAVOURED ICED TEA
HIGH NOON ICED TEA

The British tend to laugh at iced tea as some sort of American blasphemy. Of course, Popeye, being American, is a great fan of iced tea in the summer. Actually, iced tea is delicious on one of those rare hot summer days and commercially sold iced tea seems to do well – it just seems to be a shame not to make it at home! Making your own is much nicer and you can experiment with different kinds of tea such as Earl Grey and bergamot tea. Here is one using a plain tea.

Serves 6
4 large ripe peaches
3 tea bags
1 cinnamon stick
4 whole cloves
1 tablespoon castor sugar (or to taste)
6 ice cubes

Boil 750 ml water in a saucepan. Add the tea bags, remove from the heat, and add the cinnamon stick and cloves. Allow to steep for 15 minutes before discarding the tea bags. Do not discard the cinnamon stick and cloves.

Meanwhile, peel, stone and slice the peaches. Put them into a blender with 250 ml water and blend until smooth. Put the cinnamon stick and cloves into a tall 4 litre jug. Add the peach mixture then the tea mixture and sugar and stir well. Add the ice cubes and add more water if necessary until the jug is full. Stir well.

HOMEMADE PASTRY

Pastry-making looks hard but it really isn't. The thing to remember is to keep all the ingredients as cold as possible and touch them as little as possible. That is why it is better to make pastry in a food processor than by hand. Rolling it out on a work surface on which you have placed non-stick baking paper is a foolproof way of transferring the rolled out dough to the pie dish! There are several different kinds of pastry, but the two most commonly used are basically sweet or savoury. Below you will find the basic method needed for making pastry outlined. **As a general rule, any other dry ingredients should be added with the flour, and any other wet ingredients should be added with the butter.**

SAVOURY PASTRY

Basic ingredients for a 22.5 cm pie crust:
250 g plain flour
½ teaspoon salt
125 g butter, chilled
45 g lard, chilled (or vegetable shortening)

Put the flour and salt in a large bowl and add the cubes of butter and lard. Use just your fingertips to rub the butter into the flour until you have a mixture that resembles coarse breadcrumbs with no large lumps of butter remaining. This is a method called rubbing in. Try to work quickly so that it does not become greasy and stays as cool as possible.

Using a knife, stir in just enough of the cold water to bind the dough together.

Wrap the dough in clingfilm and chill for 30 minutes before using.

If you are using a food processor, put the flour, butter and salt in the food processor and pulse until the fat is rubbed into the flour.

With the motor running, gradually add the water through the funnel until the dough comes together. Only add enough water to bind it and then stop.

SWEET PASTRY

Basic ingredients for a 22.5 cm pie crust:
200 g plain flour
2 tablespoons icing sugar
75 g cold butter, cut into pieces
1 egg yolk
iced water

To make a sweet pastry, such as used in a Shoofly Pie, sift the flour and icing sugar into a bowl then rub in the butter until the mixture resembles breadcrumbs.

Beat in the egg yolk and just enough iced water (about 3 tablespoons) to make a firm dough.

Wrap the dough in clingfilm and chill for 30 minutes before using.

INDEX